W9-ASU-902

ALL TOGETHER DIFFERENT

UPHOLDING THE CHURCH'S UNITY WHILE HONORING OUR INDIVIDUAL IDENTITIES

J. Brian Tucker and John Koessler

MOODY PUBLISHERS
CHICAGO

*To the church that has been made
all together different by the work of
Jesus Christ and the ministry of the Holy Spirit.*

CONTENTS

Introduction   9

1. Our Identity Crisis   15

2. Seeing Ourselves in God's Mirror   31

3. I Am the Walrus   53

4. In with the "In Crowd"   83

5. One among Many   109

6. Race, Ethnicity, and Identity   131

7. Neither Male nor Female   153

8. Generational Differences   185

9. Living like Outsiders   209

10. Final Thoughts   231

Glossary   243

Notes   249

Acknowledgments   261

INTRODUCTION

The first words you ever spoke had to do with identity. You called your mother Mama and your father Dada—or something near the equivalent of the two. The questions you ask when you meet someone for the first time also have to do with identity. What is your name? Where are you from? What do you do? When we say such things, we are looking for more than information. We are searching for points of reference. We want to know who the other person is and who we are in relation to them.

Identity is the question of our age. It is also the root of many of our conflicts. As a culture, we are deeply conflicted about issues related to ethnic and gender identity. We are divided by age, nationality, and many other markers, even our favorite sports team.

The church is not immune from this conflict. If anything, questions of identity are even more pressing for the church because it has been made different by divine design. The church is made up of those who come from every tribe, tongue, and nation. We have been given a diversity of gifts by the Holy Spirit. We worship in a variety of styles. Most importantly, the church is made up of those whose identity has been fundamentally changed as a result of the redeeming work of Jesus Christ.

That said, you would think we would be far more

comfortable with our differences and our identity. Instead, our condition is a lot like the picture on the cover of this book. Differences are messy. They are not always fun and are not easily managed. The book you hold in your hands functions like a friend who loves the messiness of the Slinky and has some ideas for ways forward in the detangling process. *All Together Different* is about staying together in the midst of our differences rather than trying to eliminate them. Forced uniformity is not the goal of this book.

Instead, we are trying to move beyond simplistic answers by suggesting that maintaining the church's unity occurs best when our differences and unique identities are maintained in balance with what God's Word says we are. To accomplish this, we will explore contemporary research on identity formation and evaluate it through the lens of Scripture. This will allow us to suggest solutions in the form of principles that, if applied in contextually sensitive ways, can strengthen the church's unity without destroying our own individual identities. The goal is not to disentangle the church so each of us can function alone, but rather to straighten out what has become crooked so our enjoyment and usefulness can be shared with others. Slinkys are most enjoyable when played with alongside others.

Chapter 1 highlights key aspects of our current problems with identity. It focuses on identity generally, since it is often a slippery term. Chapter 2 drives home the primacy of God's Word in forming our identity. This will be crucial to understand because the cultural complexity evident in our contemporary setting requires hermeneutical precision when applying the Bible's insights. Chapter 3 looks at the concept of personal identity by introducing several key concepts of great importance for leaders. In chapter 4, we explore the vital concept of social identity. Chapter 5 deals with our most important social identity: our membership in the body of Christ. Chapters 6 through 8 examine some of the most common stress points where the church could benefit from the application of a hermeneutics of identity. Chapter 6 covers race and ethnicity, chapter 7 addresses sexual and gender issues, and chapter 8 details generational differences. Chapter 9 steps back from the messiness of those three topics to remind us that there will always be an "otherness" to our identity in Christ in relation to the world around us. This is helpful, since the temptation to assimilate is ever present.

There are no simple answers to overcoming the church's problems with disunity, but the final chapter summarizes nine principles that emerge from the book and then proposes four steps that ministry leaders and church members can take to maintain church unity in the context of our continuing and wonderful differences. At the end of each chapter, we have offered discussion and reflection questions designed to facilitate conversation and help you implement into your life the information you have received. You may want to customize these questions based on your unique settings, but they should serve as mental prompts to get you thinking about cultural and identity categories. The result of this type of thinking may produce congregations that can be all together in the midst of our differences, a delightful place of community within the indispensable yet often frustrating body of Christ.

Untangling a Slinky is a process that takes patience but is worthwhile. You might be tempted to jump to the last chapter, take the principles listed there, and just run with them. But what we are exploring in this book is more than simple quick fixes. We are pursuing cultural change.

In a recent news item, two doctors were discussing the various reasons North American society is so enamored with snack foods. One doctor described (it might be more accurate to say preached against) the ills of packaged snack foods and why he thought Americans needed to start eating apples, celery, hummus, and other vegetables as snacks. The other doctor responded indignantly, pointing out that everyone has heard this kind of advice many times before but with little effect. These kinds of suggestions rarely produce the desired change. Instead of advice, the second doctor called for cultural change, since that is what is needed first. Only a complete overhaul of cultural ideas of what constitutes a snack will change behavior. This isn't just a matter of personal taste. An entire industry, millions of dollars of mass marketing, and generations of family tradition shape people's tastes in the matter. So, the biblical and theoretical insights from each chapter will provide you with a new set of tools for engaging in cultural change, since the traditional individualistic solutions have had little effect.

When it comes to identity formation in local church settings, we face a similar challenge to those wrestling with unhealthy eating patterns in North America. Individualistic solutions are unlikely to effect change in the long term. What is needed is an approach to identity formation that understands the interrelationship between identity and theology. But there is an important order here. Identity actually precedes theology. The church's theological reflection takes place within a framework of an already-existing cultural identity. One of the functions of theological construction is to solve a group's problems of identity. In that sense, it is not theology that creates identity. An approach that begins with theology instead of identity often attempts to provide an answer to questions that have yet to be asked. The suggestion here is to listen closely to the questions being asked in the broader culture, and those questions in turn become the starting point for your theologizing, which is the case-by-case application of the results of systematic theology. What is needed is the recognition that existing social identities must be a part of the way the church's theological constructs are communicated. In other words, by paying attention to issues of identity, we are able to discern which theological constructions are best suited for clarifying those issues of identity that need to be transformed in the life of the church. Maintaining the unity of the church amid our many distinctions requires more than a generic or universalistic approach to identity. It requires a particularistic one.

It is tempting to see our existing identities as a problem or to think of them as having been erased in Christ. Many think that if we would just acknowledge our new identity in Christ and recognize that all that came before is irrelevant, then the difficulties created by the church's cultural diversity would take care of themselves. One problem with this oversimplified approach is that the cultural assumptions of the majority—no matter which culture happens to be in the majority—tend to be taken as the default approach to life. Those who are in the minority—no matter who makes up the minority—are left to wonder about their own uniqueness. Instead of freeing Christianity from culture, such an approach may actually entrench the church within the dominant culture. It is an approach that makes it easier for the church to mistake that which is merely cultural for that which is essentially Christian. So, in order to begin to disentangle the Slinky, we need clarity regarding the identity crisis that underlies our present cultural moment, since this forms the basis of the questions that are being asked—and for which this book offers hope. Grab your Slinky, and let's start untangling together.

1

OUR IDENTITY CRISIS

A few years ago, Jason Black and Frances Schroeder, a couple from New York, offered to name their third child after any brand that would pay them half a million dollars. When nobody came forward, they decided to call him Zane. A year later, a gaming company offered $10,000 to any couple who would name their child Turok, after their latest release. Nobody took the offer. One online blogger, whose personal brand was hurt because he shared the same name with a famous singer, tells expectant parents to do a domain name search before selecting a name for their child. "Could a lack of research leave your child fighting a losing battle for online visibility in the future?" he worried.[1] Long gone are the days when the only concerns new parents faced when choosing a name was the pressure of family tradition or the threat of making a choice that might eventually lead to an unfortunate nickname. It's more complicated now. A name is no longer a name. Now it's a brand.

Concern about your brand used to mean that you were either a cattle rancher or an advertising executive. Today ordinary job seekers, students applying for college, churches, and even children are branding themselves. Business management expert Tom Peters seemed to have launched the personal branding trend in 1997 with an article in *Fast Company* magazine entitled "The Brand Called You."[2] His message? You need to stand out from the crowd if you want to succeed.

But the real issue isn't branding; it's identity. When you strip away the marketing language, what you find in the typical branding exercise is really just a process of self-exploration and differentiation. *Who am I? What sets me apart from those around me? What unique value do I bring to the table that others do not?* These are questions of identity, and identity is the question of our age.

In a way, the quest for identity is really a question about our differences. Difference adds value. Yet our differences also divide us. In terms of human experience, the differences between us can be both a blessing and a curse. We live in a day when nearly every sector of our culture seems to be embroiled in an identity crisis. Its contours are revealed in the fault lines that divide us from one another: race, class, age, sex, religion, politics, and nationality. This conflict has disoriented us, both as individuals and as a culture. "After centuries of women living alongside men, and of the races living adjacent to one another, even if only notionally, our rigidly enforced gender and racial lines are finally breaking down," *New York Times* critic-at-large Wesley Morris observes.[3] "There's a sense of fluidity and permissiveness and a smashing of binaries. We're all becoming one another."[4]

But then again, maybe we're not. Morris goes on to note the widespread criticism aimed at Rachel Dolezal—president of a National Association for the Advancement of Colored People chapter in Spokane, Washington—who self-identified as an African American, despite the fact that both her birth parents were white. "Some people called her 'transracial,'" Morris explained. "Others found insult in her masquerade, particularly when the country's attention was being drawn, day after day, to how dangerous it can be to have black skin."[5] This was the same year that former Olympian Bruce Jenner changed his name and sexual identity and became Caitlin. Unlike Dolezal, who was mostly criticized for claiming an identity that differed from her birth identity, Jenner was widely praised.

WHAT SHAPES IDENTITY?

Dolezal and Jenner epitomize our current identity crisis, not only because their drama unfolded within the familiar spheres of race and sex, but also because they raise a number of fundamental questions about identity. *How is it formed? Is identity something that is given to us by somebody else, or do we get to determine who and what we are? Can our identity be changed? If so, under what circumstances?*

Race and sex are not the only factors that shape our identity. Location, family, religious persuasion, occupation, and even personal interests play a role. Many of the factors that influence our sense of identity are beyond our control. We do not originate ourselves. Someone else gives birth to us and names us. We do not get to choose our physiology from a menu of possible options—though the day may be approaching when parents may be able to do so for their children. We inherit our features from the family gene pool. We can change our place of residence once we come of age, but our most formative years are lived in locations and under conditions that are determined for us by others.

At the same time, we do contribute to a certain extent to this overall project of identity formation. Every day, we make choices that lead to experiences that can change the way we see ourselves. We also have a capacity for change. We may be born with black hair, but we can dye it blond or even pink if we choose. We may alter aspects of our physiology through surgery or prosthetics. We can move the family to a new location or forsake the family altogether. We can change our occupation or even our name.

Yet Rachel Dolezal's attempt to self-identify as an African American and Bruce Jenner's self-transformation into Caitlin make it clear that we do not all agree on which aspects of our identity are fixed and which are alterable. Many who condemned Dolezal affirmed Jenner, arguing that the categories of race and sex were radically different. "Science has largely discarded the idea that racial differences beyond superficial physical features have any basis in genetics," transgender author Evan Urqhart observed.[6] "Whether men and women differ more profoundly than racial groups do remains a somewhat contested question, but science continues to be done that supports the idea of gender differences within the human brain, while the possibility of such differences existing between races has been roundly rejected."[7]

On the other hand, *Federalist* contributor D. C. McAllister took the opposite view. "The celebration of Jenner 'becoming a woman' is a fantasy," McAllister complained.[8] "It's artificial. It's make-believe. It's not authentic at all. It's a mirage. Jenner has always fantasized that he's a woman, dreaming of the possibilities of becoming what he imagines himself to be. But possibilities in life are only fantasies when they aren't rooted in something real. You can't become a woman without being a girl, complete with XX chromosomes that determine our sex."[9]

McAllister's objection was social as much as it was biological. She argued the Jenner's male physiology and personal history removed him from the foundational experiences that shape female identity. Interestingly, those who criticized Dolezal for claiming to be a black woman did so for similar reasons. They argued that the root problem with her claim was not merely her ancestry but her inability to truly share in the African American experience.

Beyond these larger social questions, our cultural identity crisis is sparked by the more basic challenge of understanding and interacting with one another. Sociolinguist Deborah Tannen explains, "We all know we are unique individuals, but we tend to see others as representatives of groups." This kind of depersonalization is common. Tannen continues, "It's a natural tendency, since we must see the world in patterns in order to make sense of it; we wouldn't be able to deal with the daily onslaught of people and objects if we couldn't predict a lot about them and feel that we know who and what they are."[10] Identity then is not just about how we see ourselves. It is inevitably bound up with the way that others see us. This means identity is as much a function of a particular role, title, or task as it is a function of our sense of self. Some aspects of identity are more a matter of perception than being.

But Tannen warns that this tendency toward assumption and categorization, although necessary, also lends itself to oversimplification. "Generalizations, while capturing similarities, obscure differences," she explains. "Everyone is shaped by innumerable influences such as ethnicity, religion, class, race, age, profession, the geographic regions they and their relatives have lived in, and many other group identities—all mingled with individual personality and predilection."[11]

Some aspects of identity are contextually fluid. Not only can they change over time, they may "change" many times in the same day, depending upon our circumstances. The teacher who instructs her fourth grade students in the morning, eats lunch in the faculty lounge with her colleagues at noon, and then goes home to her spouse at night is the same person in each instance. But she does not interact with everyone in the same way or under the exact same identity. To her students, she is an authority. To her colleagues, she is a professional peer. To her spouse, she is a friend and lover. If she happens to have a son or daughter in class, it becomes even more complex. She may relate to her child as a teacher during school hours yet as a mother after school. The nature of her interests, obligations, and interactions differ depending upon the context.

For the person of faith, there is an additional question: What are we to make of God's role in all this? If the core of our human identity results from having been created in the image of God, it cannot be so easily thrown off. We may be able to alter or relabel some aspects of our identity, but in doing so we may put ourselves as individuals and as a culture in peril. The fact that we *can* change these things does not automatically mean that we *should*. When we take all these factors into account, the differences between us can be traced to three primary influences: divine design, human culture, and our sinful disposition.

THREE KINDS OF DIFFERENT

Divine Design

The first of these three is the most foundational. Our identity is grounded in God, and God has designed us to be different. Genesis 1:27 illustrates this fact, stating that humanity was created male and female. This biological distinction (which we will discuss in more detail in chapter 7) is the first identity marker mentioned in Scripture. It is especially significant that this physical distinction is mentioned in conjunction with the image of God. We do not reflect God *despite* our differences but *through* them. Difference is not the only thing emphasized in the creation account. Commonality is also affirmed. There is a common origin of both the man and the woman. They both come from the same source. Although the specific details of their creation differ, it is God who creates (Gen. 2:21–22). They also share the same basic nature. Adam acknowledges as much when he characterizes Eve as "bone of my bones and flesh of my flesh" (2:23). Theirs is a diversity that was expressed in unity of action as the two join together in one flesh (2:24). Additionally, they shared the same general calling. Adam and Eve reflect the divine image by exercising a shared dominion over creation (1:26). Bible scholar J. Richard Middleton has called this "the royal office or calling of human beings as God's representatives and agents in the world."[12]

Human Culture

Although men and women have been designed by God to be different biologically, most of our differences do not grow out of nature. Instead, our differences are reflected in markers such as language, values, beliefs, and customs. The word we use to refer to this second category of differences is *culture*. You don't have to go across the sea to know the difference culture makes. You might need only to cross the street. Our differences do not need to be extreme or even exotic to create cultural tension. I (John) grew up in a suburb of Detroit and lived on a block that few would consider to be culturally diverse today. My friends were white, middle-class kids like me who attended the same school and spoke the same language. We watched the same television shows (there were only three major channels in those days) and listened to the same kind of music. Yet it often seemed to me that there was a world of differences between us. I thought of my friend Larry as "Italian," even though he couldn't speak a word of the language. His parents sometimes played bocce ball. My friend Kevin was "Polish" because his family ate kielbasa. The bully next door called me a "Kraut" because my last name is German in origin. There were religious and social differences, too. Most of my neighbors were Roman Catholic. They had neatly manicured lawns, while ours was weedy and unkempt. If you looked carefully enough, you could find hundreds of little distinctions that set us all apart from one another and sometimes even set us against each other.

These differences seemed to increase exponentially after I entered junior high and high school. There, I encountered greasers, freaks, jocks, nerds, and band geeks. Although a sociologist would have said that we were all part of the same socioeconomic class, I saw it differently. The hip kids all seemed to live on the other side of an eleven-mile road. They wore the most stylish clothes and lived in cooler houses. Today, sociologists would probably say that we all were part of the "majority" culture. But back then, the majority depended upon which group you happened to be with, and most of the time I felt like an outsider or someone on the margins. The differences between us all were matters of culture.

Culture, in the broad sense, is a social construct. It is a *construct* in the sense that it is not a function of our biology. Culture is not a product of instinct or DNA, though it often feels as if it is. It is a *social* construct because it is something that must be learned and transmitted. "Culture, although it becomes for man a 'second nature,' remains something quite different from nature precisely because it is the product of man's own activity," explains sociologist Peter Berger.[13] "Culture must be continuously produced and reproduced by man. Its structures are, therefore, inherently precarious and predestined to change."[14] Culture shapes the way we see ourselves as individuals by making the group our primary point of reference. "Society, therefore, is not only an outcome of culture, but a necessary condition of the latter. Society structures, distributes, and coordinates the world building activities of men. And only in society can the products of those activities persist over time."[15] This is human work, but God's hand is also in it. According to Acts 17:26, the God who made the world also "made from one man every nation of mankind to live on all the face of the earth, having determined allotted periods and the boundaries of their dwelling place" (ESV). In this scenario, God is the prime mover. He has laid out the board and set the pieces in motion. But this is not the detached god of deism. Quite the opposite. The point is that both the unity and the diversity of human culture originate with God. Each is a part of the outworking of His plan. But there is also a dark side to this picture. A survey of history soon reveals a world of upheaval, struggle, and suffering implied in these words. When one nation displaces another, it is usually through violent means, often fueled by cultural differences. Human society's path of expansion from a single family into a multitude of tribes, peoples, languages, and nations has been a trail of tears as much as it has been a path of glory.

Sinful Disposition

The differences that set us apart may also spring from a third source. God's design and His intent for us to create culture are not the only factors. Some of our differences result from the entrance of sin into human experience. We should not overlook the fact that the first biblical record of cultural differentiation between people can be traced to an act of rebellion against God. Genesis 11 describes the confusion of languages and subsequent scattering that took place when the Tower of Babel fell (Gen. 11:1–9). This was an act of divine judgment upon those who refused to obey God's command to fill the earth (1:28). Instead, they stayed in place and attempted to build a kind of stairway to heaven that was really a monument to their own pride. Unity is not always a good thing, especially when it is fueled by sinful ambition. The introduction of cultural differences in the form of various languages was God's way of ensuring that this first human coalition would not be able to reassemble (see Gen. 11:6–8).

Babel bluntly reminds us that in addition to considering the benefits that come to us because of our differences, we must also reckon how sin affects our response to these same differences. Although many of our differences have their ground in God's design and plan for humanity, the presence of sin suggests that these same differences have as much potential to divide us as they do to enrich us. We are just as liable to find an encounter with a different culture as irritating as it is interesting. Sin can also cause us to see differences where none should exist. This sinful differentiation is the sort that Paul describes in 1 Corinthians 4:7: "For who makes you different from anyone else? What do you have that you did not receive? And if you did receive it, why do you boast as though you did not?" This is a differentiation that is driven by pride. It is the dark ambition to draw distinctions that make us feel superior to others and lord it over them.

This is why the Bible speaks of our need to be *recreated* in God's image. This is accomplished through the person and work of Jesus Christ, who is the image of the invisible God and the one who is supreme over all creation. He is the Head over all the church, and it is through His cross that we have been reconciled to God and to one another (Col. 1:15–20). Our foundational identity in Christ provides the basis for a shared experience of salvation and a common calling. This identity reconciles us in the midst of our differences. It is an identity that creates a context in which we can serve God through those differences.

Nowhere is this more evident than in the church. God has structured the church for difference. The things that distinguish us from one another make the church what it is. God has given the manifestation of the Holy Spirit to each one in the body of Christ "for the common good" (1 Cor. 12:7). The Spirit that indwells us is the same, and we share the common objective of mutual edification, though our gifts differ. Both our nature and gifting are traceable to God's design. This is the great strength of the body of Christ. We are not all the same.

There are differences in gifts, modes of service, and in the ways that we function (1 Cor. 12:4–6). There are also differences in cultural backgrounds, personal histories, and perspectives. Just as we are a community with a variety of gifts, we are a people drawn from every tribe, language, and nation (Rev. 5:9).

Our differences are more than cosmetic. Just as we all do not look the same, we all do not think the same. It is the knowledge that we have been designed for difference and have been joined to one another in Jesus Christ that enables us to look for the added value that comes to the community of believers through our differences. The obligation we have to love one another provides the motivation for disciplining ourselves to work against our sinful tendency to marginalize those unlike us. The church provides a context where we can recover from our individualistic nearsightedness and learn how to live in community. Our interconnectedness to one another in the body of Christ and the equipping of the Holy Spirit teach us to "have the same care for one another" (1 Cor. 12:25 ESV). Through Jesus Christ, God the Father will achieve what those who attempted to build the Tower of Babel could not. In the fullness of time, He will "unite all things" in Christ (Eph. 1:10 ESV).

A SMALL WORLD AFTER ALL?

Diversity is good, but it isn't always comfortable. Adapting to the challenges that come with our differences is not easy. One of the greatest problems we face is the tendency to minimize the trouble our diversity often creates for us. Because we live in an age that values diversity, we tend to romanticize it. "In this age of the shrinking planet and the global village, we all know the world is composed of an enormous variety of peoples and that their beliefs and practices differ from our own in every conceivable manner," cultural communications expert Craig Storti observes.[16] "Cultural diversity is a truism, even a cliché, of our time."[17] As a result, we expect our encounters with the "other" to be like a Disney ride: relatively brief, mostly entertaining, and with minimal to no discomfort. We expect some differences in appearance and style, but we also believe that in the end everyone will be singing the same song. It turns out that we are wrong. Our well-meaning naïveté does not prepare us for the common irritation and emotional exhaustion that comes with dealing with our differences. The expectation that we are basically on the same page with those who are not like us keeps us from preparing to face our differences. We assume that everyone thinks like we do and shares our most important values. When we learn they don't, we are shocked, dismayed, and often offended.

We have been conditioned since childhood to operate this way. The centripetal force of every human culture pressures us to conform. Divergence from the accepted standards of the group is discouraged in every culture and is often punished. Although the phrase "majority culture" is mostly used pejoratively today, it is the normal bent of every culture to desire that its values, preferences, and practices be the standard for others. The fundamental assumption of all human interaction is that everybody sees the world just as we do. "This assumption, which we are rarely, if ever, aware of, is the foundation and operative principle of much of human behavior," Storti explains. "Indeed, if all of us did not live by this conviction, most human interaction would not be possible."[18]

Once we understand our own cultural assumptions and recognize the problems created by our fallen human nature, we begin to understand why some of our most painful experiences take place in the church. We find that the same differences that God designed to add value to us often divide us. It is no accident that the church's first major conflict fell along cultural lines. This ethnic dispute erupted when a complaint by the Hellenists arose against the Hebrews because their widows were being neglected in the daily distribution (Acts 6:1). The Corinthian church divided over the way its members had been gifted by God. Some began to develop a sense of inferiority, believing their gifts were less valuable than others' (1 Cor. 12:15–16). Others, however, felt superior because they believed they had been given more prominent gifts, and they even excluded those they deemed inferior (1 Cor. 12:21). There were party differences. Some aligned themselves with key leaders in the church in a way that dismissed others (1 Cor. 1:12). There were also class differences in the early church, which caused it to divide along the lines of the "haves" and the "have nots." The wealthy were shown special favor, while the poor were treated with contempt (James 2:1–4).

What is the solution? The first step is to recognize that our identity is anchored but not static. Identity is multidimensional and contextually fluid. It begins with what is given to us by God, both in terms of nature and through the Spirit. Yet it is also shaped through ordinary human development and personal experience. Because our sense of identity is subject to various conflicting influences, we must be discerning about which voices we allow to name us. And since we are talking about *human* identity, we must be prepared to face the collateral damage that sin has wreaked upon this aspect of our nature. We must also be willing to engage the subsequent struggle that comes from dealing with others whose sense of identity has been similarly affected.

Before we can deal with our identity crisis, we will need to break out of our pattern of denial. The presence of sin in human experience guarantees that our common diversity is both beautiful and messy. Difference adds value, but it also creates problems. We have mixed feelings about the things that set us apart from one another. Sometimes we deny that our differences matter. At other times we draw battle lines because of them. Our differences are complex and more subtle than we often recognize. But the good news is that the things that distinguish us from one another do not have to set us against each other. The work of Christ and the ministry of the Holy Spirit enable us to be many and one at the same time. This is what it means to be the church. We are not altogether different. We are all *together* different. The various parts of the body of Christ have been knit together into one. We do not have to work through our identity crisis alone. The God who has called us by name from eternity past has also sent Jesus Christ to die on our behalf in order to redeem our identity. He has given us the Holy Spirit to remind us of both our calling and our equipping. Because of this, we are able to say with the apostle Paul, "By the grace of God I am what I am, and his grace toward me was not in vain" (1 Cor. 15:10 ESV).

Questions for Reflection

1. Where does your sense of identity come from? How much control does a person have over their own identity? How much should they have?
2. How much of our identity should be fluid, and how much should be fixed?
3. How do other people shape our sense of who we are? When is this good, and when is it problematic?
4. Most Christians recognize that cultural diversity strengthens the church. Why, then, do we struggle with cultural diversity so much?
5. What challenges come with diversity? What are the limits for diversity in the church?

SEEING OURSELVES IN GOD'S MIRROR

A commercial for Ancestry.com features a man named Kyle who describes how the company helped him discover his true ethnic identity. "Growing up, we were German. We danced in a German dance group. I wore lederhosen," Kyle explains. But after submitting a DNA sample, Kyle was shocked to learn that he wasn't German at all. "Fifty-two percent of my DNA comes from Scotland and Ireland, so I traded in my lederhosen for a kilt!"

We may laugh at Kyle's story, but it raises a serious question: What *really* makes us who we are? Is it our DNA? Is it only our perception? Or is it something else? Clearly some aspects of identity are shaped by biology. Our birth parents determine our sex and ancestry. Kyle didn't choose his DNA; it was given to him at conception. In this respect, his "Scottish" identity was fixed before he ever became aware of it. Yet Kyle's DNA did not give him a Scottish brogue or a taste for haggis. Was he less Scottish when he was wearing lederhosen and doing German folk dances? How exactly did a DNA report make him Scottish? The answer is that it changed his self-perception.

Perception is intrinsic to identity. We are who we see ourselves to be. In many respects, our sense of identity is a mirrored reflection. We know who we are as a result of what others tell us about ourselves. But identity is also projected. The identity that is reflected back to us is often an image we project to others. Those who knew Kyle before he learned of his Scottish heritage probably thought of him as German. Image is not all there is to identity. Image is often skewed and may even be false. Yet image is essential both as a feature and a function of identity.

IMAGE AND IDENTITY

Image is the inner vision we use to define ourselves or what we hope to project to others. Image is the ideal that is brought to mind when we think of the labels or categories that define who we are. What does it mean to say I am a man or woman, a parent or a child, an employee or a citizen, or even a Christian? The imaging feature of identity provides an inner model or stereotype that shapes the way we view ourselves and behave. We usually think of stereotypes as pejorative, and they often are. A negative stereotype offers an overly simplified and/or destructive picture of a person or group. The ideal image I have of myself may not correspond with reality or may be impossible to attain. But the inner image to which I aspire can also be good, accurate, and within my reach. Self-stereotyping is necessary for developing a sense of group identity. It is one of the things that gives the group its sense of "groupness." We identify with the group because we see ourselves in one another. Yet before this can be true, we must agree about what it is that we are looking for.

Image has to do with the ways we show the world who we are or who we want them to think we are. When Kyle learned of his Scottish identity, he "traded in his lederhosen for a kilt." Discovering this new identity changed the way he presented himself to others. If identity is about *being*, image is about *showing*. This means that image is essentially symbolic in nature. The artifacts, actions, and characteristics we use to project image are merely emblems that point to something else.

The symbolic nature of image makes it possible to create a false or misleading image. I can manufacture an image that makes me appear to be something I am not. I can manage my image so I don't appear to be what I truly am. I can use image to disguise myself or to hide what is embarrassing about my true identity. The way we sometimes use social media is an obvious example of this. The social network isn't just a means of connecting with friends. It is a tool we use to create, curate, and project an ideal image of ourselves. Whether it's the cartoon avatar we use to identify ourselves when commenting on someone's blog or that carefully staged photo of ourselves looking spontaneous that we post on Instagram, social media is used to craft a public image.

But the practice of projecting an idealized image is nothing new. In *The Road to Character*, David Brooks tells how Dwight Eisenhower used image to lead more effectively by adopting an exaggerated persona. Eisenhower lived by what Brooks calls a kind of "noble hypocrisy," suppressing the less admirable aspects of his character and presenting a different disposition to his followers. "He was not naturally good at hiding his emotions. He had a remarkably expressive face," Brooks explains.[1] "But day by day he put on a false front of confident ease and farm-boy garrulousness. He became known for his sunny, boyish temperament."[2] Eisenhower would later employ this same studied affability as president. "As president, he was perfectly willing to appear stupider than he really was if it would help him perform his assigned role. He was willing to appear tongue-tied if it would help him conceal his true designs."[3]

This malleability makes us suspicious of image. We like to think our identity is natural and static. It's who we are and it remains consistent all our lives, we assume. It is the "self-created and self-sufficient, highly centered 'true inner person,' persisting through time and standing above the vacillations and shifting relationships that characterize day-to-day living."[4]

In this view, we are like containers for the self. We carry our identity with us wherever we go. No matter what the context or the role, who we are is constant.

Image seems to be the opposite of this. We think of image as manufactured and therefore false. We deem the person who presents multiple faces to others, depending on circumstances, to be insincere and maybe even deceptive. We call someone whose inner self diverges from one's outer person a hypocrite. Consequently, when most of us think about our own identity, we think of a single self. It is the same face that we present to everyone at all times. But this isn't how identity works. We do not present a single face to those around us, but many faces. Our identity is not a single self but rather is made up of many selves depending upon the context, nature of the relationship, or the circumstance in which we find ourselves.

THE STORY OF OUR IDENTITY

The sense we have of who we are changes with time and experience. Philosopher Charles Taylor notes that identity has a narrative quality. We discover who we are by paying attention to our own story—where we've been and where we're going. We do not come into the world with a cohesive sense of identity that remains fixed all our lives. Nor is identity instantaneous. It develops progressively. "It is not only that I need time and many incidents to sort out what is relatively fixed and stable in my character, temperament, and desires from what is variable and changing, though that is true," Taylor explains.[5] "It is also that as a being who grows and becomes I can only know myself through the history of my maturations and regressions, overcomings and defeats. My self-understanding necessarily has a temporal depth and incorporates narrative."[6] In other words, we know who we are by attending to our own story.

You'd think this would be easy. It is *our* story, after all. And as far as our experiences go, we are always at the center of them. But precisely because it is our story, we find it difficult to follow the plotline. Because we experience the story from the inside, we lack the objectivity of a reader.

Anne Lamott's observation about the plot of a writer's unfolding novel is true of our own lives. It unfolds slowly and lacks clarity at times. Lamott writes, "Your plot will fall into place as, one day at a time, you listen to your characters carefully, and watch them move around doing and saying things and bumping into each other."[7] The plot builds to a climax, and the climax is all about change. We know this is also true of our lives, but we are fuzzy about the details. We agree with the apostle John's observation: "Dear friends, now we are children of God, and what we will be has not yet been made known. But we know that when Christ appears, we shall be like him, for we shall see him as he is" (1 John 3:2). We have the big picture in mind, but the minutiae along the way often confuse and frustrate us. Sometimes we're tempted to conclude that the details of the larger plot are moving in the wrong the direction. Like Jacob, we're tempted to say, "Everything is against me" (Gen. 42:36). Often, the story of our lives does not unfold as we imagine it will.

We would like to believe our identity is our own personal possession. It is the secret, inner self that belongs to us alone. We may share it with others, but it does not belong to them. Yet Charles Taylor notes that identity is actually communal. We do not develop identity in isolation. As he puts it, "We achieve selfhood among other selves."[8] Some aspects are given to us at birth. Others are added through experience. If it weren't for my children, I could not think of myself as a parent. Without a wife, I cannot be a spouse. I need students in order to be a teacher. Without electors, a president is just a politician. Some aspects of identity diminish with time and may even be laid aside. I was not always a professor. If my spouse dies, I may marry again or remain single.

There is also the question of significance. Not everything that shapes my sense of identity is equally weighted. Some things have more gravity than others. The fact that I may be a Trekkie is not as important to me as the fact that I am a parent—unless I happen to be attending a Star Trek convention with my children in tow. Certain aspects of my identity are so foundational that they influence me my whole life. Others are peripheral, occasional, and temporary. This does not automatically make them unimportant, but it does make them transitory. Then, there is the question of who actually determines the weight of each aspect. There was a time when society or the church did this for us. Today we believe identity should be self-constructed.

In 1936, Edward VIII abdicated the British throne to marry American divorcée Wallis Warfield Simpson. In his address to the nation announcing his decision, he declared, "I have found it impossible to carry the heavy burden of responsibility and to discharge my duties as King as I would wish to do without the help and support of the woman I love." Constitutional crisis for England ensued. But for Edward, it was an identity crisis. He wasn't choosing a relationship so much as he was selecting a role for himself. Simpson had already been his mistress for two years, but Edward wanted her to be recognized as his wife. He also wanted to escape his royal duties, which he often described as a "job" that he hated.

Our actions usually do not make world headlines in the way that Edward's did, but every day we make similar identity-forming elections and abdications. We choose to act out one role instead of another. A husband may accept his duties as a spouse instead of the appeal of going out with his friends on a Friday night. The boss may give her employees a large assignment with a short deadline, and they may find themselves focusing on their job instead of their families. Or maybe we decide it is better to obey God than the government, setting aside our identity as a citizen of one nation in favor of our citizenship in the kingdom of heaven. We wear a multitude of faces each day, yet none of them is exactly a mask.

LOOKING IN THE MIRROR

Facing so many pressures and options, where do we find a clear sense of what our real identity looks like? The answer is that we must find it in the mirror of God's Word. Like Edward VIII, we too have royal duties to consider. Jesus Christ "has made us to be a kingdom and priests to serve his God and Father" (Rev. 1:6). We are named by our parents and given nicknames by our friends. We get a sense of who we are as others reflect our own image back to us. But it is God who has shaped our identity at its most fundamental level. He is the one who has given us a new birth and a new identity. This identity is reflected to us through the Scriptures. Just as we rely on a mirror to reflect our own image back to us, we are dependent upon God's Word to show us who we really are.

New Testament professor Klyne Snodgrass describes this as an interpretive act, calling it a hermeneutics of identity. "Scripture is about identity formation," Snodgrass explains.[9] "In the end the whole discussion about the authority of Scripture is about identity. Do we allow Scripture to tell us who we are and who we are to be, or do we give that authority to something else?"[10] But what does Scripture actually say about your identity?

First, it tells us there is something in our identity that corresponds to God. The two terms that the Bible uses for this are *image* and *likeness*: "Then God said, 'Let us make mankind in our image, in our likeness, so that they may rule over the fish in the sea and the birds in the sky, over the livestock and all the wild animals, and over all the creatures that move along the ground' " (Gen. 1:26).

Rather than describing this identity as the personal and

unique possession of the individual, Genesis 1:26 makes a sweeping statement about all humanity. We have been created to be a reflection of God, and this dimension of our identity is *not* self-determined. It has been defined for us by God as a result of His creative act. Just as a child does not get to choose which parent he or she will resemble physically, so we are made, not self-made.

Some have argued that the divine image is something in the makeup of human beings. Our capacity to reason is the prime example of this. Others have suggested that the image is relational. Those who have been created in God's image have been created for relationship—with God and one another. Still others see the divine image as a matter of function. The image is something we do. Specifically, it is the exercise of dominion. We have been created in God's image in order to rule or exercise dominion over the rest of creation. This sets human beings apart from the rest of creation and at the same time establishes a relationship between us and creation. Humanity's vocation also establishes a relationship with God. And our rule over creation is one of stewardship, not domination. Human beings have been created in God's image in order to represent His interests as they live in the world He created and owns.

While the language of "ruling" denotes stewardship, it also communicates the idea of royal supervision. The psalmist confirms the royal nature of humanity's vocation in Psalm 8:5–8, when he echoes Genesis 1:26, describing this dominion as a kind of crowning. But the dominion of Genesis 1:26 is also the language of service. This is the role of a royal steward, someone who has been appointed to act on behalf of the king and look out for his interests. It is the kind of work the slave Joseph did on behalf of Pharaoh. It involves the exercise of authority, but it is delegated authority.

Dominion is granted to Adam and Eve, but the domain in which they exercise dominion belongs to God. The realm of their responsibility is described as being "over the fish in the sea and the birds in the sky, over the livestock and all the wild animals, and over all the creatures that move along the ground" (Gen. 1:26). This places humanity on another level when compared to the other creatures. Human beings are more than smart animals. Our human identity leans more in the direction of God and the angels than it does in the direction of the fish, birds, and livestock. This difference is reflected in Adam's first act of dominion, naming all the animals (2:19). Up until this point, God was the one naming creation (Gen. 1:5, 8, 10).

We should not think of this naming as a childish exercise, the sort of thing a mother might do with her toddler while looking through a picture book. It is more like the studied contemplation of a scientist or philosopher. The conclusion of Adam's careful reflection is summarized in Genesis 2:20. There was no "suitable" helper for Adam to be found among them. The Hebrew word expresses the idea of that which is in front of or before. The chief purpose of this exercise seems to have been to prepare Adam for the creation of the helper who would share dominion with him. Of all the creatures God had created, only the woman corresponds to him. This means that our identity has a sexual component to it, as was discussed in chapter 1 and will be discussed again in chapter 7. God's Word reveals that the reflection of the divine image is expressed in the complementary polarity of male and female.

YOU ARE WHAT YOU DO

The responsibility of dominion places human identity within the framework of vocation. When we meet someone for the first time, one of the first questions we usually ask after learning their name is "What do you do?" Adam and Eve were created for a vocation and were designed to fulfill it together. Eve's creation was directly related to their mutual calling, according to Genesis 2:18 and 20. Both Adam and Eve were included in the Genesis 1:28 mandate to "fill the earth and subdue it." There is more in view in this command than simply populating the planet with offspring. It also involves more than tending the garden. This command to fill the earth and subdue it points to the development of human culture, what Andy Crouch (following Ken Myers) has described as "making something of the world."[11] This activity is both creative and interpretive. It involves both the creation of things and the investment of those things with meaning or value.

Work is not merely what we do to earn money. Indeed, much of our vocational activity may not even be for pay. Sometimes, like Paul the tentmaker, our employment is the work we do that enables us to fulfill our vocation. But it is doubtful that Paul approached his work as a mere side job. He was always a Christian first. Paul did not step out of his Christian calling when he took up the task of tentmaking. Just the opposite. He makes it clear in 2 Thessalonians 3:8–10 that the one served the other. Paul worked "night and day" not in order to accumulate wealth but so he would not be a burden to the church and so he could be a role model to Christians prone to idleness.

While we are more than our work, our work is an important

41

aspect of our identity. Work, as the Bible describes it, has a functional dimension. By our ordinary work, we provide for ourselves and for our family (2 Thess. 3:7–12; 1 Tim. 5:8). This kind of work has value and meaning, but it is not an end in itself. Jesus teaches that a person's life is not summed up by what they accumulate (Luke 12:15). Nor is our value to God and the world around us based on what we are able to produce. God values my work, to be sure, but my value in God's sight is not based on my career achievements. This is what separates the biblical idea of vocation or calling from the secular notion of a career.

Vocation is a calling from God to an activity for which we have been empowered by Him. A career is something else. Career is a matter of employment and self-achievement. In a career, one has to be useful—as the employer defines *use*—in order to be of value. In a calling, the obligation is to be faithful. In a career-oriented culture, work becomes a kind of religion. Everything we are and do serves the job. If we take a break from our work, it is not really for our own sake. It is only so that we will serve the job better. For the person whose sense of self is shaped by this kind of thinking, identity is determined by performance. I am what I do, and that is all that I am. For those who are career-oriented, identity is also often a function of comparison. Workers compete with one another. The most productive are valued most. I determine my worth by comparing my output with yours. The more I achieve, the better I feel about myself. I feel even better when I know that my performance has outstripped someone else. A biblical view of identity, however, is shaped by a different orientation. It is the orientation of grace.

SIN'S EFFECT ON IDENTITY

Grace is essential to identity because the image we see of ourselves in Scripture is not altogether attractive. While the Bible tells us we have been made in God's image, it also shows us how that image has been shattered. The cracks that we see when we look at ourselves in God's Word are not cracks in the mirror but flaws within ourselves. Adam and Eve were created in God's image and likeness, but they were unfaithful in the execution of their mandate. Adam fell into sin through disobedience, and all humanity fell with him (Gen. 3; Rom. 5:12). Sin has put us at odds with our original identity. As a result, both our status with God and disposition towards Him changed.

One of sin's most devastating consequences has been its effect on human perception. We no longer have a clear view of God. This is not because God has made Himself more obscure since Adam's fall. God continues to reveal Himself through creation as He has done since the beginning. It is our response to this revelation that has obscured our view. Instead of seeing clues about God's eternal power and divine nature in what He has created, sinful humanity has redefined God and deified creation itself. Sinful humanity "exchanged the glory of the immortal God for images made to look like a mortal human being and birds and animals and reptiles" (Rom. 1:23). By exchanging the truth about God for idolatry, humanity distorted not only the idea of God but also its own image in the process. No longer satisfied with its calling to image God, humanity aspired to take God's place, just as Satan did.

The cultural effect of this distortion moves in two directions. On the one hand, it tends toward an exaggerated view of humanity, in which we see ourselves as more than we are. This is the tendency toward self-deification. In some cases, this is explicit, reflected in the claims of those who say that we are all gods. More often, it is less overt. We don't claim to be God, but we essentially put ourselves in the place of God by following our own will. We do this whenever we set aside His standard or redefine His will based on our own personal preference.

Ironically, this sinful self-perception is equally liable to move in the opposite direction. Instead of seeing ourselves as more than we are, we see ourselves as less. This distortion does not see humanity as created in God's image and likeness but merely as an animal and maybe even less than an animal. Instead of viewing humanity as the "crown of creation," this perspective considers human beings to be a biological accident. Humans are merely winners of an evolutionary lottery that has granted them temporary preeminence. It is a form of self-loathing.

Sin is spiritually debilitating. The Bible uses the word *dead* to describe those affected by it (Eph. 2:1). To be spiritually dead is to be at odds with God and ourselves. Spiritual death causes us to love ourselves more than God, but in a self-destructive way. For the spiritually dead, sin is a way of life inclined toward harmful self-gratification. This does not necessarily mean that everyone who is spiritually dead is debauched, but it does mean that we are caught up in our own desires. Indeed, we are so caught up in sinful desires and thoughts that the Bible uses the analogy of slavery to describe our predicament. Like an addict who returns time and again to that which has stolen everything that was once precious to him, those who are spiritually dead willingly and repeatedly subject themselves to the cruel mastery of sin. Paul describes this self-destructive cycle in Romans 6:20–21: "When you were slaves to sin, you were free from the control of righteousness. What benefit did you reap at that time from the things you are now ashamed of? Those things result in death!"

Sin changes the nature of our relationship with God by making us His enemies. Although it is popular to anthropomorphize God and speak of Him as "the man upstairs," the reality of our position as sinful humans is far more alarming. God is no doting grandfather who winks at the foibles of His unruly grandchildren. The Bible describes Him as a "consuming fire" (Heb. 12:29) and warns, "It is a dreadful thing to fall into the hands of the living God" (10:31). In Scripture, the reaction of sinful humanity to the presence of God is always the same: even those who are the most holy and the most devoted to Him dare not treat God as an equal. They do not give Him a thumbs-up, high five, or round of applause. Instead, they fall down on their faces in fear (Gen. 17:3; Num. 14:5; Ezek. 1:28; Rev. 1:17).

Adam's initial reaction when becoming aware of God's presence after his disobedience was to hide (Gen. 3:8). Ours is the same, only our mode of hiding is more subtle. We do not hide among the trees but behind our own rationalizations and fantasies (Rom. 1:21). We reconfigure God's image and adjust His standards so that they are more palatable to our tastes. We explain away those aspects of His truth that make us uncomfortable. The result is a more manageable god, one who has been recast in our own image and likeness. This god agrees with us. He exists to cater to our whims. Or perhaps he regards us from a great distance with a detached attitude of benign neglect. Either way, he is no threat to us.

Yet deep within us there remains a disquieting challenge to these assumptions, a discordant voice among our usual inner chorus of self-approval. We're not always aware of it, mainly because we don't like what it says to us, and so we suppress it. It tells us that the world is not as we imagine it. Nor are we as we imagine ourselves. If we listen to this inner voice—perhaps we should borrow the language of the courtroom and call it a witness—it will suggest that God is not the amiable person we have imagined Him to be. He is quite different. In fact, He is a Holy Terror (see Gen. 31:42). "That is the terrible fix we are in," C. S. Lewis observes.[12] "If the universe is not governed by an absolute goodness, then all our efforts are in the long run hopeless. But if it is, then we are making ourselves enemies to that goodness every day, and are not in the least likely to do any better tomorrow, and so our case is helpless again."[13]

Lewis is right. Our plight as the Scriptures depict it is helpless, but it is not hopeless. The reason it is not hopeless is precisely because we *are* helpless. There is another force in play that has the power to awaken us from our spiritual denial and change the dynamic of our relationship with God. It is grace. Of all the factors that shape a Christian's identity, none is more important than grace. Only the grace of God can redeem our perception of Him and ourselves. It is God's grace, bestowed upon us by the person and work of Jesus Christ, that restores us to a right relationship with Him and renews our true image.

Before we explore the change God's grace introduces into our thinking about ourselves and our relationship with God, we are wise to recognize three important facts about grace. First, grace is all about what God does. The apostle Paul makes this clear when, after describing our position as those who are by nature the objects of divine wrath, he explains the intervention of grace: "But because of his great love for us, God, who is rich in mercy, made us alive with Christ even when we were dead in transgressions—it is by grace you have been saved" (Eph. 2:4–5). Grace is grace because it involves God's initiative. This is not about us finding a way out of our spiritual dilemma by means of cleverness or even as a result of moral renewal. According to Paul, God interjected His grace into the equation while we were yet dead in our transgressions. The dead cannot do anything for themselves.

Second, grace does not reflect divine ambivalence or a kind of split personality on God's part. Grace is not a matter of Jesus quieting His overly excitable and easily angered Father. It is not God's gentle self somehow overcoming and overruling His angry self. The Bible's depiction of God as a consuming fire and a source of terror does not tell us everything there is to know about God's nature or His disposition toward us. This holy God has great love for those who were made in His image. This has been true from the very beginning. Indeed, the implication of Scripture is that God created Adam, knowing in advance the events that would ensue and the measures that would need to be taken to reclaim humanity. Grace was in view even before Adam was created. Jesus is the "Lamb who was slain from the creation of the world" (Rev. 13:8). Grace was not a grudging concession on God's part. Nor was it a last-minute pass intended to fix His plan for creation after the wheels unexpectedly came off. Grace was God's plan from the beginning. This was implied from the very start, when God replaced the makeshift garments Adam and Eve had pieced together for themselves with garments of skin that He made for them (Gen. 3:21).

Third, grace sets those who receive it apart from the rest of humanity. God's love and grace do not mean that He will turn a blind eye to those who persist in their self-delusion. The experience of grace is contingent upon faith in Christ (Eph. 2:8). Grace is a gift. It is something that we receive. But just what is it that we receive? It is not merely a set of facts about God and His Son Jesus Christ. The language that the Bible uses to describe grace is fundamentally relational. John 1:11–13 gives a short synopsis of Jesus' life and ministry: "He came to that which was his own, but his own did not receive him. Yet to all who did receive him, to those who believed in his name, he gave the right to become children of God—children born not of natural descent, nor of human decision or a husband's will, but born of God." To receive the grace of God, we must receive Jesus. To receive Jesus, we must accept Him as God's promised Messiah and the only acceptable sacrifice for our sin. Only those who do receive Him can rightfully claim to be God's children. What is clear from John's short synopsis is that not everybody falls into this category.

This is the fundamental change that grace introduces into our thinking about ourselves and our relationship with God. Because of grace, our status toward God changes from outsider to insider. We cease being His enemies and are restored to our true position as His sons and daughters. And there is change that is both radical and mysterious, a change in our spiritual location. Paul describes it in Ephesians 2:6 as enthronement. We have been raised up with Christ and seated with Him in the heavenly realms. Actually, the primary location that Paul identifies in this verse is not in heaven but in Christ. By His grace, God has united us with Jesus Christ in His entire redemptive work. Just as we were united with Adam in his sin, so we who have experienced God's saving grace have been joined to Jesus Christ in His life, death, and resurrection. This is not a mere formality or a theological fiction but a vital reality that changes our relationship to sin. Theologian Marcus Johnson explains, "In our union with him, Christ's death and resurrection are the redemptive realities through which the dominion of sin is overcome in us and we are restored to newness of life."[14]

This union has the power to reconfigure our identity. It changes not only how we are able to live but also who we are. This is the point the apostle seems to be making in 1 Corinthians 6:9–11 (ESV). He begins by describing the kind of person who will not inherit the kingdom of God: the sexually immoral, idolaters, adulterers, men who practice homosexuality, thieves, the greedy, drunkards, revilers, swindlers. He then makes this bold statement: "And such were some of you. But you were washed, you were sanctified, you were justified in the name of the Lord Jesus Christ and by the Spirit of our God." This is more than a "don't do" list for recovering pagans. It is a declaration of new identity. "You were this," Paul says in effect, "but no longer."

Why did Paul feel it was necessary to say such a thing? Given the moral criticisms Paul makes of Corinthian behavior in the surrounding chapters, it seems unreasonable he was congratulating them for reaching moral perfection. It is more likely that he was reminding them of their new identity, precisely because some of them had succumbed to some of the very things he lists as being incompatible with a lifestyle marked by the kingdom of God.

Union with Christ is instantaneous, but the subsequent transformation of life that it effects is not. A changed identity is foundational to a changed lifestyle, but many aspects of that change take time. Our spiritual growth sometimes feels as if it takes place in fits and starts. There may even be times when we go backward like the Corinthians. The time frame for this process is not a few weeks or months but our whole lives. The general trajectory is in the direction of conformity with Christ. One of the effects of living in a world obsessed with image management is that it makes us susceptible to a kind of false perfectionism. We confuse the manufactured image with reality. We are intolerant of the shortcomings of others and blind to our own failures. But God's agenda in the gospel is not image management or even image creation. The aim of the gospel is restoration. We put aside the sinful practices of our old life the way someone lays aside soiled clothing. We exchange those for a new self that is "being renewed in knowledge in the image of its Creator" (Col. 3:10).

IDENTITY AS AN ACT OF ATTENTION

Paul's reminder to the Corinthians of their past was not meant as a dig. It was intended to focus their attention on reality as God defines it, to give us a proper vision. It turns out that perception really is the key to identity. If you see yourself as German, you will think you are German. You may decide to wear lederhosen or learn German folk dancing. If you see yourself as someone who continues to be enslaved to sin, you will not think you have any other alternative but to comply when the allure of sin beckons you. Our identity is a spiritual fact, as certain as Kyle's Scottish DNA. But it also requires an act of attention on our part. The Christian life is a matter of Spirit-empowered practice as well as status-altering grace.

God's Word gives us critical metaphors and symbols upon which our convictions should be based, and our behavior should be shaped by those convictions. We are no longer what we once were. We do not yet know what we will be in its entirety. But we do know this much: We have been joined to Jesus Christ by faith and subsequently to one another. Although we may continue to feel the effects of the sin that still dwells within us, we know that its back was broken at the cross. It seeks to assert its tyranny on us, but it is no longer our master. We have traded our old rags for robes of righteousness.

Occasionally, we forget these facts. At other times, our own failures—whether big or little sins—make these truths difficult to believe. On those occasions, we must not only work to see ourselves differently but also work to make that seeing become a fixed and lasting vision. There is more to this than patterns of practice. Indeed, it does not really begin with practice. Instead, it is a habit of memory. Just as the church trains to focus its attention upon God when it gathers for worship, we must also develop the habit of seeing ourselves in the mirror of God's Word. None of us really knows who we are until somebody else tells us.

Questions for Reflection

1. Would your friends say that your identity on social media matches who you are in person?

2. Which has more influence on your identity: DNA or self-perception?

3. How does image contribute positively to identity, and how can it mask identity?

4. How much of your sense of identity is shaped by what you do?

5. What problems come from seeing your work as central to who you are?

6. How does the truth that you are an image bearer of God change the way you see yourself?

7. In what way is identity an "act of attention"?

3

I AM THE WALRUS

The song *I Am the Walrus* by the Beatles famously begins, "I am he as you are he as you are me and we are altogether." Although it wasn't what John Lennon had in mind when he wrote the song, the lyrics describe fairly well the way identity works. I am "me" to myself and "he" to the other person. Personal identity is grounded in distinctiveness. I am not you. You are not me. Identity is also grounded in similarity. We understand who we are by noting what we hold in common with others. This is a continual process. It is also a contextual process. Although we often speak of personal identity in the singular, it is more accurate to think in terms of multiple identities. These identities may shift based on changing situations and differing group memberships that are important to us in a given setting (like the teacher/wife/mother we mentioned in the last chapter). While our individual experiences lead us to reflect on who we are internally, this reflection is also social.

There are several ways to study personal identity, but for the purposes of this book, we will limit the scope by taking this definition of personal identity: it is "an individual's knowledge that he or she is different from other people (group members) together with some emotional and value significance to him or her of this sense of individuality."[1] This definition builds on something called self-categorization theory (which we will discuss in more detail later). But before we look at the processes associated with personal identity, let's unpack the concept of personal identity more generally. Keep in mind that a key goal of this book is to honor our unique identities while seeking to maintain the unity of the church.

THE ROLE OF FAITH

Identity is the sum total of factors that relate to and form a person. According to theologian Klyne Snodgrass, it includes our physical and mental characteristics, history, relationships, commitments, and boundaries.[2] It is also a series of ongoing processes and self-interpreting memories that are wrapped up in a specific perspective about the future.[3] We will unpack these characteristics below. However, one of the most significant influences on our identity is sin, something that the Beatles' description of identity fails to take into account. This is important to keep in mind because a significant amount of spiritual formation occurs outside of the four walls of the church, and all too often church attendees integrate wrong views of sin into their view of the world. For leaders, this is important to keep in mind. It challenges leaders to help their congregation think theologically about their engagement with the spiritual messages they receive from popular culture.

What the Beatles could not communicate clearly is that sin is the reality that infiltrates our identity. Sin—that propensity to self-centeredness—fragments and fractures our relationships and ourselves in classic Voldemortian fashion. As we think about disentangling our messy relational world, we shouldn't run too quickly past the role of sin. Sin produces an alternative internal dialogue that creates theological and practical problems. One instance in which the Beatles *do* pick up on this issue is in the song "Eleanor Rigby," which highlights one of the effects of sin: loneliness. Paul McCartney's query as to "where do they all come from?" is repeated throughout the generations. Relational distance, both vertical and horizontal, may be traced back to sin. The sorrow of loneliness caused by sin is seen in Lamentations 1:1–6, for example, where Jeremiah laments the fall of Zion, a city once packed with people but now desolate. The good news, however, is that while sin is part of our identity, it doesn't get the last word. What Paul McCartney couldn't tell Eleanor Rigby or Father McKenzie in the midst of the consequences of sin, Jeremiah reveals in Lamentations 3:22–23: God is faithful, and His loving-kindness never ceases.

As Christians, the reality that transforms our identity is faith. It allows us to hear the truth of God's Word as it defines our realities and dissolves our false identities. Faith eventually allows us to walk through our relational world without the masks that we all too often keep close at hand. From an identity perspective, faith is what happens to our thinking processes when we encounter the truth about God and His perspective on who we are. This work of the Holy Spirit breaks our existing thought patterns and begins to reshape our false identities, those aspects of our worldview that have led us to a lack of human flourishing.

Identity-transforming faith is not some nebulous feeling.

It is a response to the triune God, as Paul wrote in Galatians 2:20: "I have been crucified with Christ and I no longer live, but Christ lives in me. The life I now live in the body, I live by faith in the Son of God, who loved me and gave himself for me." The "no longer live" and the "life I now live" form the two poles that shape the landscape upon which the eight characteristics of identity interact. When we consider the following eight characteristics, we need to remember who we once were when sin dominated our lives and who we are now in Christ. This will help us to better understand ourselves. Yet knowing these characteristics helps us to do more than simply understand ourselves. It also helps us understand others. If we are going to live together in the context of our continuing differences, each of these characteristics needs to be considered and understood.

EIGHT CHARACTERISTICS OF IDENTITY

1. Our Physical and Mental Characteristics

Our identity is based on our physical and mental characteristics. This reality is shaped through various processes that include the way we think, our level of emotional connectedness, and our interaction with those around us. Physical characteristics are one of the key factors that tell people who they are. Consider the apostle Paul. The New Testament hints at what his appearance may have been like (see 2 Cor. 10:10), but the second-century work *The Acts of Paul and Thecla* gives us more information, describing him as short and bald with crooked legs and eyebrows that met. While the work is apocryphal, its description still points to the way one's physical appearance contributes to his identity.

Similarly, one's mental characteristics—the ability to reflect on oneself—is a particular characteristic of being human. Paul points to this when he declares, "But by the grace of God I am what I am" (1 Cor. 15:10). Paul's subjective sense of who he was, his awareness as to what made him different, is highlighted here in this verse. God's grace, his gift to Paul, formed the basis of Paul's self-understanding. Physical and mental characteristics are part of what it means to be created in the image of God (Gen. 1:26–27), so it shouldn't surprise us that these are central to identity. These factors come together in embodiment, an idea that will be developed further throughout this book. The main point here is to remember that our bodies are not our own; they belong to Christ (1 Cor. 6:19–20).

2. Our History

Our history contributes to our sense of who we are, as we discussed in the previous chapter. People exist in the context of a story, a narrative that gives orientation. This history can be problematic when trying to live in community with other Christ followers. For example, church conflict often has both a "presenting problem" (the initial symptom of the larger issue) and an underlying problem. Divisions over church budgetary matters that seem insignificant to leadership may stem from deep-seated distrust based on financial mismanagement in the history of the church before the arrival of the current pastor, and these past stories may continue to influence their current thinking and behavior. The historical details of a church fight based on financial mismanagement make it necessary to re-align aspects of our story going forward. Our true history is the history of Christ, into whom we are grafted. His history, within which and under which our personal history is subsumed, is our defining history. What will we allow to define us? This is the key identity question. Our histories do not change, but the way we interpret them can. Our histories are to be remembered and processed for truth. These stories occur within a particular culture and local context. This is a necessary ingredient for our Christian identity. But it is not ultimately determinative. The goal of following Christ is not to escape our histories, cultures, and contexts, but to learn the unique way that God has laid out for us to follow Christ. In that sense, Christian identity is not theologically bound but open ended.

3. Our Relationships

Our relationships also contribute to our sense of identity. This is seen most acutely in our historical families. The family unit serves as the basic building block for our sense of self, but the influence of families is not always positive. It can also contribute significantly to deformations of identity.

Parents usually have culturally conditioned ideas concerning the type of person their child should be. Jesus experienced such a conflict (Mark 3:31–35). He reprioritized the kin group around the idea of the family of God (see also Eph. 2:19–22). For believers, our relation to God in Christ is the primary defining force for our identity. The body of Christ is the fundamental metaphor (see further chap. 5). Thus, Christian identity is not an individualized affair, even though it emerges from an individual relationship with Christ. Jesus did not repudiate family relations in Mark 3. Rather, He emphasized the way doing the Father's will impacts one's existing relationships.

This is evident in cross-cutting social dilemmas, those "me

versus just us versus us all" moments we sometimes experience. Imagine there's a parent who is in an important meeting at work. The parent receives a text message stating a family emergency has occurred. The work and family relational contexts, which were previously working harmoniously, are now in conflict. What action will the parent take? Ignore the text? Leave the meeting? The higher category in the identity hierarchy will determine the action. If the parental role is salient, then the person will leave. If the employee role is higher in the hierarchy, then the person will stay in the meeting and hope to resolve the issue at another time. The challenge for Christ followers involves knowing how to determine specific courses of action when Scripture makes a claim on our identities. Yet our social setting often makes it difficult to know the way to apply that claim.

4. Our Commitments

Our commitments reveal a significant amount of information about our identity. The following is a quick list of potential commitments: (a) to a location; (b) to investments of interest, time, and money; (c) to oppositions; (d) to attitudes, perceptions, and opinions; (e) to activities we are assigned or choose—our worship, entertainment, and work; (f) to the icons or heroes we choose; or (g) to the people we seek to impress. These commitments are not bad or sinful. They themselves are neutral, but they do reveal our sense of self.

One example from this list can be highlighted here. In the New Testament, we see a continuing commitment among Jesus and His followers to Israel's restoration. Jesus points to this in Luke 13:35: "Blessed is he who comes in the name of the Lord." This citation of Psalm 118:26 in its context points to an expectation of a future restoration for Israel in the land (see also Rom. 11:25–26). This is to be expected since Israel's scriptural tradition located its rebirth in its ancient land generally and in Jerusalem specifically (Zech. 12:10–13:1; Ezek. 36:24–37). The earliest Christians expected this restoration, and that expectation became an important part of their identity. Yet in contemporary theological debates, one often hears claims that the land of Israel has lost its theological significance with the coming of Christ. For example, Gary Burge writes, "Early Christian preaching is utterly uninterested in a Jewish eschatology devoted to the restoration of the land."[4] This is not just an obscure theological debate. It has significant political and social implications. A commitment to a location is not incompatible with the lordship of Christ. What is true with regard to our commitment to a location is true in all our commitments; by the power of the Spirit, we must work to reprioritize these commitments so as to not diffuse our in-Christ identity.[5]

5. Our Boundaries

Our boundaries also make known our identity. Understanding who we are in Christ involves a constant process of putting some boundaries up and removing others. The first boundary is conversion itself. This marks the beginning of the new creation spiritually, but the embodiment of that newness is a process (2 Cor. 4:16; 5:17). So in many ways, Christian identity is about boundary setting. The New Testament writers did this as they addressed issues of ethnicity (Gal. 3:28), geography (Matt. 28:18–20), past associations (Eph. 4:17–24), and ethics (Col. 3:9–11).

Just as in the first century, today some boundaries are

already set for us by our culture. But as Christ followers, we do not necessarily recognize those boundaries—such as boundaries between races, or limitations on forgiveness. The concerns and implications of boundaries involve all aspects of Christian identity. In our contemporary setting, boundary marking often comes with a bent towards legalism, as different groups within the congregation express their understanding of the social implications of the gospel. While the purpose here is not to resolve these differences, one way forward is to look at these debates through the lens of identity. What limitations should be placed on identity? Based on Paul's teaching in 1 Corinthians, our limitations should primarily be organized around the following four areas: immorality, idolatry, unscriptural thought patterns, and cultural boasting. A more expansive way of describing this would be to follow Paul's counsel in 1 Corinthians 10:31: "So whether you eat or drink or whatever you do, do it all for the glory of God."

6. Our Fluidity

Our identity is not fixed but is continually formed in a life of growth, continual renewal, and being changed from one stage of "glory" to another (2 Cor. 3:18). This means that leaders need to pay attention to the implications that our conversion has on bodily practices within the congregation. Paul seems to be addressing such a concern in 1 Corinthians 8–10 with regard to food offered to idols. This suggests that identity maintenance is crucial to the church's work in worship and education, since there is an ever-present temptation for congregations to think they have arrived at a resting place in their corporate life. Thinking about identity formation as a process can help us avoid frozen identities. Frozen identities have occurred at different times throughout history. In Europe, for example, the medieval political establishment mindset contributed to churches functioning as a symbol of national identity that was then unable to adjust to new realities. As a result, the majority of these national churches have lost influence in today's post-secular setting. These majestic cathedrals serve as reminders of the need for identity maintenance in changing cultural settings.

7. Our Self-Interpreting Nature

Our identity involves a series of self-interpreting memories. Christian identity is an internal, reflective journey where we remember and interpret who we are. The Bible reinforces this by emphasizing the priority of sincerity of heart and faithfulness. Spiritual disciplines are ways for our minds to remember, interpret, and reform the identity that God has for us. The Lord's Supper and baptism also are significant identity-shaping acts based on identification with our risen Lord. The interaction between self-description (who I understand myself to be) and community-description (who those in my local church understand me to be) is important, since the individual and the community both are part of the body of Christ. Identity is found in what God says, and this is tested by the interaction of self and community.

8. Our Future Orientation

Our identity has a future orientation to it. Our view of the future tells us something about ourselves, who we will be and where we are going. Death is not the end of our identity. God's future for us continues to define us. Our belief in the future bodily resurrection impacts our identity, which in turn directs our ethical choices. We can see this in Philippians 3:17–21, where those who are "enemies of the cross" have destruction as their destiny; but for those in Christ, their "citizenship is in heaven," and when He returns, Christ "will transform" their "lowly bodies . . . like his glorious body." Here, Paul relies on the future-orientation of Christian identity to address current ethical practices within the community (see also 1 Thess. 4:13–18). Our vision of our future identity has significant impact on the ethical choices we make.

When I (Brian) was an undergraduate student preparing for pastoral ministry, my vision to be a pastor someday influenced certain decisions I made. Of course, others did the same, even though I didn't appreciate their future identity the same way. For example, there were several "polyester preachers" on campus. They wore suits and carried briefcases to classes (and meals) because they were convinced that doing so was integral to their pastoral identity. While my vision for pastoral attire was more casual, our respective clothing choices signaled our understanding of pastoral identity. My problem was I didn't fully appreciate their unique calling, which would in the future lead them to minister to a segment of our culture that I likely wouldn't be able to reach. We need diverse expressions of pastoral identity in order to reach people with the gospel. Keeping our eye on our resurrection future with God can transform our thinking about our differences and help us appreciate more fully the diverse ways in which people embody their calling and vocation.

These eight factors of identity are important since they are the points where our differences become most obvious in church settings. Recognizing their complexity helps us overcome reductionistic approaches to Christian identity that offer simplistic solutions to complex problems. In order to understand better what is involved in the formation of identity, we need to explore some of the processes that researchers have uncovered about this shared human experience. However, before we look at these, we need to highlight the centrality of being in Christ, since it serves as a master identity as we seek to overcome disunity in the church.

OUR MASTER IDENTITY

Paul uses the phrase "in Christ" three different ways to describe the formation of a master identity. First, he uses it in an objective manner, referring to "the redemptive act which has happened 'in Christ' or depends on what Christ is yet to do."[6] Second, Paul also uses it in a subjective way to describe Christ followers. In this category, we might place discussions concerning the social implications of the gospel or the outworking of the objective aspects of Christ's redemption. Third, he uses it to refer to his own ministry and mission. These references address Paul's social identity, which includes his Jewishness, apostleship, and ongoing relations with members of the Christ movement. Thus, Paul's use of the phrase "in Christ" is differentiated and requires attention to context in order to discern which aspect is being emphasized in a particular passage.

Paul employs all three nuances of what it means to be in Christ as a master identity in 1 Corinthians, a letter crucial for understanding the church's unity amid differences. The objective aspect of God's grace given in Christ is evident in 1:4. This was the foundation and framework for the Christ movement's identity. The difficulty for the Corinthian church was to understand how being in Christ was to define and shape their existing identities. Thus, Paul used the phrase "in Christ" in a subjective sense to teach them about their ongoing sanctification and life in Christ (1:2, 30), and to provide correction (3:1; 4:10). Paul also uses the phrase "in Christ" as an ingroup/outgroup label in the shaping of their identity. In 4:15, the phrase functions as an implicit critique of Roman educational and imperial ideology, while in 4:17, it is used in a manner following the contours of Jewish pedagogy, which was Paul's preferred way of instructing Christians. For Paul, "in Christ" is a key corporate ordering principle that integrates the objective work of Christ, the subjective experience of believers, and the ongoing ministry of the church within a framework of identity.

To be in Christ is inherently social and focuses on building a community. James Dunn notes, "Likewise we can hardly avoid speaking of the community, a community which understood itself not only from the gospel which had called it into existence, but also from the shared experience of Christ, which bonded them as one."[7] Here, he comes close to the idea of a salient in-Christ identity. Notice Dunn points out the centrality of both calling and the gospel in the formation of the community. It's plausible that a misunderstanding about the nature of both of these had contributed to the instability of the church in Corinth.

It seems, however, that the Corinthians were not bringing their cultural identities under the lordship of Christ. For example, 1 Corinthians 7:20 and 24 indicate a misunderstanding about the nature of calling and, by extension, the nature of the continuation of identity in the context of that calling.

Also, 15:1–2 reveals that the Corinthian Christ followers still didn't understand the basic structure and content of the gospel. Thus, Paul restates the basic framework of the gospel as well as a number of the social implications that follow from accepting the gospel message (15:3–11). The gospel and God's call are vital to Paul's understanding of community formation in Christ.

Dunn also suggests that the experience of being in Christ connects believers corporately and socially. This doesn't mean there isn't an individual component to being in Christ. W. D. Davies remarks, "The formula which Paul most frequently used to describe the nature of the Christian man was that he was 'in Christ' . . . In short 'in Christ' is a social concept, to be in Christ is to have discovered true community."[8] Thus, being in Christ was a way for Paul to describe the unity of those in the church. For some reason, the Corinthian church was not functioning harmoniously, leading to its destabilization (1 Cor. 1:10–12). For Paul, being in Christ is the believer's overarching or master identity, a position that does not obliterate other existing identities but reprioritizes them. Paul is an example of this in that his Jewish identity remains salient as he continues his mission among the gentiles (1 Cor. 9:19–23).

Identity salience is one way to describe the objective and subjective aspects of being in Christ. *Salience* relates to the way in which various identities interact based on changing social circumstances. A salient identity is one that is activated in a given situation. It emerges from its previous location lower in the identity hierarchy and begins functioning as a master identity. A Christ follower, for example, may be on a break during a business meeting, and one of her colleagues mentions a struggle she is having in her marriage. She just heard of a good book on marriage from her pastor's recent sermon. In that moment, she needs to decide whether she will take the risk and mention it or keep the conversation at the surface level by ignoring it. If her Christian identity is salient, she should take the risk.

Paul's aim is to see a salient identity of being in Christ form in his audience. This identity results in the formation of a new culture in which the community lives out the social implications of the gospel. As Davies notes, "There is a social aspect to the Pauline concept of being 'in Christ'; union with Christ however personal had meant incorporation into a community that could be described as one body."[9] Thus, being in Christ is an objective experience that is lived out subjectively by the Christ community, which is part of God's mission to redeem the world.

William S. Campbell notes that diverse expressions of an in-Christ identity are expected in a particularistic approach in contrast to the universalistic approach that downplays diversity, difference, and the continued relevance of social identities in Christ.[10] If church members are going to remain united while honoring their respective God-given differences, then they should be taught about both the objective and subjective components of being in Christ and their relevance to discipleship and contextually sensitive gospel communication. Ideas for how to accomplish this will be highlighted in subsequent chapters. For now, let's return to two key processes researchers have uncovered as to the way identity is formed.

TWO KEY PROCESSES
OF SELF-CATEGORIZATION

British social psychologist John C. Turner developed a theory of the individual known as *self-categorization theory*. It built on the earlier theory known as *social identity theory*, which we will discuss in detail in chapter 4. The subtitle for this book emphasizes the importance of upholding the unity of the church while honoring our individual identities. Turner's research is especially helpful in this regard because he was concerned with *how* individuals are able to act as a group. This raises important but often overlooked questions. How does a collection of individuals form into a group? How do individuals define themselves as they become part of a collective? How does being part of a group, like a church, affect an individual's behavior and existing relationships? Turner's research uncovered two processes that contribute to this: self-categorization and depersonalization. It is important for us to understand these two processes as we live among fellow believers with different backgrounds and identities.

In order to understand the way this works, we first need to know the categories that the group uses to define itself—called "ingroup" categories. Most churches have a doctrinal statement or statement of belief. Ideally, this document outlines practices that cue individuals in on what one does to enter and continue being a part of the group. So, church attendees begin to perceive themselves in terms of similarities and differences that they share in contrast to others. This provides a sense of belonging and identity.

There are many different categories any group might use to do this: sex, age, ethnicity, kin, occupation, or religion. These characteristics are also affected by one's social context. My sex or age tells me something about who I am as an individual. But when there are two or more people, this self-understanding is also shaped by the culture of the group. A new church plant, for example, may value young single adults differently than does an established congregation. This begins the process of group formation. These individuals see themselves in light of shared ingroup perceptions.

This brings to the fore the important idea of self-categorization, which is "the process of perceiving the self as an interchangeable member of a category that is defined at a particular level of abstraction (personal, social or human)."[11] Seeing myself as a person places me in a larger category than simply male or female. In that case, then, "person" is the higher level of abstraction. Taking this idea further as a Christian, recognizing that I am a part of the body of Christ—which is our most important identity—places me in an even larger category (a higher level of abstraction) than simply a member of the local church. The mirror of God's Word tells us that for believers, being in Christ is the highest level of abstraction and forms the basis of full inclusivity among the group.

This means that all other personal identities should be nested under our identity as a Christian. Think of a Russian nesting doll. As each smaller doll fits within the largest one, so each lower-level identity of ours fits within the larger one, our identity as a member of the body of Christ. In this approach, therefore, my identity as a businessperson is shaped by my Christian identity.

The second process that Turner uncovered is "depersonalization," which is "the process of self-stereotyping by means of which the self comes to be perceived as categorically inter-changeable with other ingroup members."[12] This is connected to self-categorization and the way a person recognizes that they are part of a particular category. What is crucial here is that people start moving away from defining themselves in light of their individual differences. This does not require a loss of per-sonal identity or the submergence of the self into the collective. Depersonalization does not function like the Borg from Star Trek, the cybernetic organisms linked in a hive-like fashion to the collective mind. Instead, certain situations call for an ad-justment from the personal to the social level of identity. The content of information used to determine who we understand ourselves to be is transformed to a higher level of abstraction and inclusivity. This is an addition to our existing identity, in which actions can now occur based on similarity and difference.

Imagine a pastor and an elder who enjoy playing golf to-gether. Now imagine them in a board meeting together where conflict erupts. As golfers, they enjoy each other and develop strong relational bonds. They see each other as sharing the same sporting passion. When they are in board meetings and the elder continues to challenge new ideas put forth by the pastor, the pastor becomes somewhat confused. He assumes that since he had been building a personal relationship with the elder in question, he would likely go along with the pastor's new initiatives. What's going on?

The confusion clears somewhat when we apply the theories mentioned above. It's likely that some level of depersonaliza-tion is occurring—that is, the elder is seeing him as a category (a pastor) and not a person. The elder views the pastor in a way that places him in an "outgroup." Maybe he has unresolved conflict with the previous pastor that is influencing his current behavior. The elder may not even be aware of this, and simply building more personal relationships will not resolve the issue. The wise pastor recognizes that the process of depersonalization is occurring and works with the elder to resolve the difficulties. This is more of a process than a one-time event. Resolution progresses gradually as unresolved conflict continues to spill over into existing ministry settings. Self-categorization and depersonalization are not processes that go away; they are part of the way the brain functions. The challenge for ministry leaders is to overcome lazy categorization and depersonalization habits. This requires vulnerability and generous hospitality to those with whom we differ.

This book is about the way personal identity works itself out in church settings. Issues related to group formation are crucial in resolving congregational conflict. We need to be aware of self-defining categorizations and the way in which they function in the various groups that make up the congregation. This was also a key part of Turner's theory, in that he was interested in uncovering the circumstances in which certain identities become salient, ready to be acted upon.

Now imagine a mother who is hosting a birthday party for her small daughter. Grandma and Dad are standing next to her as she lights candles for her daughter to blow out. Children from the neighborhood are seated at the table with their parents. How does this woman see her identity? Without thinking much about it, she will probably take on several identities during the course of the party. To her daughter, she will be a mother. But to the grandmother, she will be a daughter. To her husband, she will be a wife. But to the other children, she will be a host. To some, she will be a neighbor. Yet in all this, she will also have a separate identity that is uniquely herself. These combine to form an identity hierarchy, which shifts based on the situation.

We believe that being in Christ must consistently be in the top position in the hierarchy in order to inform and direct different identity performances. The uniqueness of the mother's identity in the above illustration is what Turner means by self-categories. In different situations, different categories will be more or less important to us. Even in a single situation, several of these identity nodes, to use the imagery from computer networks, might be activated.

The wise leader seeking to maintain unity within a congregation will become an archaeologist of people's identities. One way to do this is to start a conversation by asking people to list twenty words that describe who they are. The Indiana Jones of identity will pay attention to the circumstances or the various aspects of the person that might be contributing to the formation or deformation of their Christian identity. However, doing this may prove to be quite a challenge. Let's see how Paul tried to handle categorization in 1 Corinthians 4:1–5 so we can gather insights for the challenges associated with identity-based approaches to unity in the church today.

1 CORINTHIANS 4:1–5: WEAKNESSES IN SELF-EXAMINATION AND SELF-CATEGORIZATION

In 1 Corinthians 4:1, Paul provides specific guidance regarding the thought processes of the community by essentially saying,

"Think of us this way." He offers two major categories for doing this: "servants of Christ" and "stewards of the mysteries of God." These references to Paul's earlier discussions (2:1, 7, 3:5 ESV) reinforce the group's perception of who Paul was and the way he originally proclaimed the gospel among them. In the few years since he had founded the Christ group in Corinth, Paul seems to have been replaced as a prototype—the leader who embodies the group's beliefs—by other teachers whose ministry was shaped by different values. So, Paul offers these two categories as a reminder of who he was and how he functioned as an apostle.

Then in 4:2, he reminds them of the group norm by emphasizing accountability: "moreover, it is required of stewards that they be found faithful" (NIV). This is how they should view Paul. Yet "steward" is also the category they should use when thinking of themselves. However, Paul's reminder also raises the possibility that a steward might not be trustworthy. This kind of judgment language is frequent in this portion of the letter (see also Gal. 2:17), and Paul reestablishes a group norm of trustworthiness that will characterize Timothy as a group prototype in 4:17.

As church leaders, thinking of ourselves as stewards can be helpful in a number of ways. First, it offers a biblical alternative to the corporate CEO model that has taken root in many churches. Second, it reorients our thinking about the people we serve, reminding us that the group we lead belongs to God (see 1 Peter 5:2). Paul reminds us in 1 Corinthians that we, as stewards, are called by our King to be trustworthy while we await His return.

In 1 Corinthians 4:3 (ESV), Paul's argument takes an unexpected turn. He speaks of the community's evaluation of himself but also says, "With me it is a very small thing . . ." We might have expected Paul to emphasize the importance of the community's assessment of him. Instead, he minimizes it: ". . . that I should be judged by you or by any human court." This describes two types of social influence and power, one that operates within the community of faith and one that is controlled by those outside (6:1–11 NIV). Clearly, this issue is important to Paul, since he uses the same word for "judged" twice in this verse and once in 4:5. He provides a concrete application of his teaching in 2:14–15 that those outside the community do not have the knowledge to properly assess communal life within the Christ movement, while those within the community of faith are not subject to the evaluation of others.

However, Paul takes this a step further in 4:3 when he declares that he does not even "judge" himself. His own self-categorizations and assessments are not trustworthy forms of evaluation either. In this one verse, Paul has called into question three of the primary means of identity formation: the individual (in this case, Paul himself), the ingroup (those within the Christ group), and the outgroup (the Roman Empire represented by the law courts). Paul is not confident in the ability of any of these to properly assess the social implications of the gospel (see also 1 Cor. 2:14–15; 4:3–4). Later, he does temper this assertion. In 1 Corinthians 9:3 he lays out his defense for those who will examine him, and in 10:25 and 27 he provides guidance for judgments concerning meat offered to idols (and adds the resources of one's "conscience"). Judgment is given a missional component in 10:27 and 14:24. There, Paul guides the Corinthian Christ followers in the way judgment about "outsiders," those who are part of a subgroup defined as "unbelievers," functions. For

Paul, judgment and self-examination—what Turner's identity approach describes as self-categorization—are important concepts in the formation of an in-Christ identity, but they have also allowed problems to enter into the community.

Let's pause here and think about how practical and timely Paul's instruction is for us. He offers guidance for how the church is supposed to think. As a pastor, I (Brian) found myself in far too many church meetings where the proposed solution to a problem was guided by secular thinking. Now this isn't to argue that important leadership or economic principles can't be gleaned from social science. Much of this book does just that. But this material has to be subservient to Scripture. God's Word must guide the way we appropriate truths from these other resources into day-to-day ministry practices.

Returning to the biblical text, we find in 1 Corinthians 4:4 that Paul offers himself as an example, declaring, "I am not aware of anything against myself" (ESV). Improper self-assessments had adversely impacted communal life within the Christ movement, so he quickly adds, "But I am not thereby acquitted." Paul recognizes that he is incapable of accurately assessing himself, and if those in the assembly follow his example, they will likely think less of their own ability to properly assess their identity practices as well. Paul then focuses the Corinthians' categorizations upon the One on whom the community is founded: "It is the Lord who judges me." So, judgment is brought up again, and it is the Lord who can be relied on to properly assess their communal life.

By pointing to the Lord's judgment, Paul shifts the time frame from this age to the age to come. The sphere of judgment also shifts from the present social situation to a future context in which their future social identity, the one Paul seeks to create, will be evident. This future-oriented identity is even more clearly expressed in 1 Corinthians 4:5: "do not pronounce judgment before the time" (ESV). The Corinthians overidentified with the political power of Rome and its present power to judge, leading them to minimize any significant role for future judgment. This is not to argue that the community had a full-blown "over-realized eschatology"—one that assumes God's judgment is already being played out in the present—but an "over-identification with Roman imperial eschatology."[13] Earlier in this letter, Paul expressed his lack of confidence in the Corinthians' ability to appropriately evaluate the social implications of the gospel (1:10–12; 2:5; 3:1, 18), so he now instructs them to wait until "the Lord comes." The Lord is the only one who can accurately judge the community and its leaders, their internal motivations, categorizations, and identifications. Yet rather than using this insight to demoralize the group, he reminds them that "each one will receive his commendation from God." This reorients the time frame for the congregation and adjusts the relative importance they place on the way they currently see themselves. A transformed approach to social comparisons informs their identity performance as they await their future "commendation from God."

OUR ULTIMATE SELF-CATEGORIZATION: GOD'S CHILDREN

Paul recognized that categorizing within the Christian community is risky and likely to misconstrue reality from God's point of view. Social psychologist and theologian Christena Cleveland notes that thinking about these challenges can be discouraging, and so she offers practical steps to help transform our thought processes with regard to categorization. First, she says we need to make our categorizations conscious. Once we are aware of their existence, we can foil their negative influence. By the empowerment of the Holy Spirit, we can override enculturated negative categorizations, such as those associated with gender, race, ethnicity, or age (all of which will be discussed later in this book). Cleveland concludes, "We must relentlessly attack inaccurate perceptions in our everyday interactions, weekly sermons, denominational meetings and dinner table conversations. . . . Rather than continuing on as cognitive misers who lazily rely on inaccurate categories to perceive others, we need to engage in . . . *cognitive generosity*."[14]

Cognitive misers often emerge during church meetings. They are the individuals whose spiritual gift is to say, "No!" They always have reasons why the church can't move forward or why a new ministry initiative won't work. Or they may think that any ministry change would somehow go against the doctrinal purity of the church. Both of these issues—perpetual negativity and confusion over doctrine and practice—contribute to church disunity and are examples of cognitive miserly thinking. Leaders who are going to help churches maintain unity in the context of difference need to cultivate new ways of thinking among the group, described by Cleveland as cognitively generous ways of thinking. One way to do that is to help the group see themselves as a kinship group.

We need to begin seeing ourselves through another identity characteristic. We must begin seeing ourselves as God's children (1 John 2:28–3:10). There are several ways God describes our identity in His Word, and one that is particularly helpful for our purposes here is our identity as His children. Let's briefly look at 1 John 2:28–3:10 through a hermeneutics of identity.

The big idea in this passage is that confident children of God continue to live rightly. Living into an identity as God's children gives us confidence in relation to Christ's second coming: "Now, little children, abide in him, so that when he appears we may have confidence and not shrink from him in shame at his coming" (2:28 ESV; see also 3:3). It also gives us security in our rebirth: "If you know that he is righteous, you may be sure that everyone who practices righteousness has been born of him" (2:29 ESV). This verse highlights the boundary-marking function and processual nature of an in-Christ identity. It also reminds us of the existence of our new family at conversion, which should lead us to be passionate about our adoption: "See how great a love the Father has bestowed on us, that we would be called children of God" (3:1a NASB).

These are crucial identity-forming verses! We really are God's children. Thus, we are separate from the world (3:1b), yet there we are still going through a process that won't be completed until Jesus returns (3:2). So, confident children of God continue in purity (3:3) because they (a) have hope and (b) are becoming conformed to the image of Christ. As we see our identity as God does—that we are children of God—we will live rightly (3:4–10). Living out this identity means that we love God (3:4–7) and love people (3:8–9). First John 3:10 summarizes the individual and communal aspects of what it means to be identified as God's children: "By this the children of God and the children of the devil are obvious: anyone who does not practice righteousness is not of God, nor the one who does not love his brother" (NASB). Kinship discourse was a central identity strategy in the New Testament, and it is a key way our Christian identity is formed today. Thinking of ourselves as God's children is vital for the formation of an in-Christ personal identity that is ready to be acted upon in any given situation.

When I was pastoring I had a deeply committed and active leader in the church who asked if he could speak with me one day. So we met, and after a bit of small talk, we got to the key issue: his personal identity crisis. I was initially taken aback by this sudden turn, since he was a missionary veteran, and here he was coming to a young, new pastor for counsel on an issue I'd likely be coming to him to discuss. What he said next has stuck with me for a long time: "Pastor, I feel like I'm a soldier under orders rather than a child under God's love."

I don't remember much of the other details of our discussion, but since then I've often seen similar patterns of life among Christians, especially those heavily involved in ministry. There are many metaphors in Scripture describing our union with Christ, and I'm not suggesting that our soldier identity doesn't have its place. But a key resource in the formation of our Christian identity is the biblical truth that we are God's children. How do we know if we are beginning to see our personal identity through the lens of being God's children? There are various ways of thinking about this, but let me offer just a few.

First, children of God recognize that they belong to God. Not only that, they recognize that other Christians belong to God as well (see 1 Cor. 3:23). This will decrease the likelihood of judgmentalism within the church, since all are recipients of the same grace (1 Cor. 15:10a). Second, children of God start to see non-Christ followers not as the enemy but as victims of the evil one (1 John 5:19). This truth gives us a new sense of empathy for the struggles of nonbelievers (see Eph. 2:1–3; Matt. 5:9). Third, seeing ourselves primarily as God's children rather than soldiers under orders ultimately provides us with a new motivation and empowerment for serving God and carrying out His commands (1 John 5:2; Rom. 8:14). Finally, seeing ourselves as fellow siblings helps disparate groups in the church to maintain their unity. Being in Christ is both the *theological* and *social* center for life within the church. It gives us a shared identity now and a goal to move toward, to become increasingly unified while we maintain our respective differences—which are good creations of God (Gen. 1:31). However, there is more to identity than the personal side. There is also a social component, a topic to which we now turn.

Questions for Reflection

1. Popular media has a powerful effect on cultural attitudes toward ethnic and sexual identity. What are some ways it has affected you negatively?
2. How has your family background been a positive or negative influence on your identity?
3. How can seeing yourself as part of God's family re-orient your perspective on your personal history?
4. We usually think of stereotypes as being bad. How can stereotypes shape a group's sense of identity for the better?

5. The Corinthians were trusting in Rome's power for their security. Where do you see Christians relying on political power to fix society's problems? Is there anything wrong with this?
6. How should the future shape a Christian's identity?

4

IN WITH THE "IN CROWD"

In 1964, singer Dobie Gray performed "The In Crowd," in which he states that he is "in with the in crowd" and goes wherever that crowd goes and knows whomever that crowd knows. This song highlights the precise nature of *social identity*, which is "an individual's knowledge that he or she belongs to certain social groups together with some emotional and value significance to him or her of this group membership."[1] Gray's song is all about the benefits of being popular. Being in with the in crowd involves preoccupation with knowing the newest practices and the right language of the cool group. The singer promises a future of love and everlasting bliss if the object of his desire will simply follow him to the in crowd.

Being part of the in crowd isn't confined to hipsters and high schoolers. It is a concern for the church as well. The apostle John makes a condemning observation about those who opposed him: "They went out from us, but they did not really belong to us. For if they had belonged to us, they would have remained with us; but their going showed that none of them belonged to us" (1 John 2:19). This us/them language is a reminder of the role that a group has in shaping our identity. Group identity is based on a kind of double vision. It is shaped by comparing myself to those who are part of the group to which I belong or wish to belong. It is also shaped by contrasting myself to those outside the group. When I compare myself to those in the group, I am basing my self-evaluation on a group norm or prototype. This prototype is usually positive. It is a picture of the ideal member, and the Beatitudes (Matt. 5:3–12) give us such a picture. When I contrast myself to those outside the group, I calculate the benefits of being with the in crowd against the liabilities that would come from being an outsider. Most of the time, these comparisons are of specific attributes such as age, sex, education level, religious belief, ethnicity, or social class. Both evaluations are important aspects of group cohesion. There can be no inclusion without exclusion.

The interplay of social identity is the primary area in which church conflict arises. Because of this, we first need to briefly highlight key components of social identity theory, since having an awareness of these processes will help us overcome those tension points that work against church unity, especially in light of subgroups like the "over-churched." Second, we will highlight the role belief plays in social identity and survey the centrality of the gospel for identity in 1 Corinthians. Third, we will introduce the importance of roles, hierarchies, and a master identity, while illustrating how these influenced a small group of Christians in Nazi Germany. Finally, we will conclude by returning to 1 Corinthians and the way social identity was important for Paul's guidance and mission in Corinth.

WHAT SOCIAL IDENTITY THEORY IS

Henri Tajfel, a Jew who survived the German prisoner of war camps because he was thought to be a French and not Polish Jew, developed the theory known as social identity theory. He was primarily concerned with intergroup conflict and the factors that engender negative group behaviors. He was particularly interested in discovering why so many enculturated German Christians could participate in the Nazi atrocities. He found that social categorization and depersonalization (described in the previous chapter) were central to this quest. Comparing ingroups and outgroups highlights the differences between "us" and "them" and thereby contributes to the formation of our social identity. These social comparisons bring to the fore the important role of leadership in shaping the group prototype, which combines the ideal traits of a group member. This understanding helps to explain the existence of stereotyping and differentiation between various groups that may otherwise appear to have much in common in terms of language, sex, ethnicity, or religion.

This theory contrasts previous ideas that focused on individualistic understandings for behavior and conflict. According to social identity theory, behaviors are indicative of a specific social or group identity that is prioritized at a given moment. This identity, along with the situation in which it occurs, determines the socially acceptable behaviors of a group. Central to the research is a specific understanding of a group "as a collection of individuals who perceive themselves to be members of the same social category, [and] share some emotional involvement in this common definition of themselves." But a group also "achieves some degree of social consensus about the evaluation of their group and their membership in it."[2] This evaluation is based on group beliefs and occurs at both the interpersonal and intergroup level. It takes more than numbers to make a group. There must be a sense of "us" and "them."

This sense of "us" and "them" can be illustrated by a well-known joke written by Emo Philips some thirty years ago:

> Once I saw a guy about to jump off a bridge. I said, "Don't do it!" He said, "Nobody loves me." I said, "God loves you. Do you believe in God?" He said, "Yes." I said, "Are you a Christian or a Jew?" He said, "A Christian." I said, "Me, too! Protestant or Catholic?" He said, "Protestant." I said, "Me, too! What franchise?" He said, "Baptist." I said, "Me, too! Northern Baptist or Southern Baptist?" He said, "Northern Baptist." I said, "Me, too! Northern Conservative Baptist or Northern Liberal Baptist?" He said, "Northern Conservative Baptist." I said, "Me, too! Northern Conservative Baptist Great Lakes Region, or Northern Conservative Baptist Eastern Region?" He said, "Northern Conservative Baptist Great Lakes Region." I said, "Me, too!" "Northern Conservative Baptist Great Lakes Region Council of 1879 or Northern Conservative Baptist Great Lakes Region Council of 1912?" He said, "Northern Conservative Baptist Great Lakes Region Council of 1912." I said, "Die, heretic!" And I pushed him off.[3]

The mere existence of group identity can lead to ingroup and outgroup stereotyping and conflict. Cleveland rightly registers a concern here: "numerous Christians who tend to gravitate toward churches that are filled with people who look, talk, worship, think and experience life like them are unaware of the dark side of division."[4] Many Christians don't recognize that group membership actually alters their self-concept. It moves them from a distinct personal identity that distinguishes them from others in relation to their attitudes and memory to a collective identity with its own set of cognitive, evaluative, and emotional dimensions. This group membership allows group action to take place.

The premise of social identity "is that belonging to a group ... is largely a psychological state which is quite distinct from that of being a unique and separate individual, and that it confers social identity, or a shared/collective representation of who one is and how one should behave."[5] It focuses on the following aspects of communal life that are often seen in congregations:

(a) intergroup behavior
(b) stereotyping of people
(c) intragroup behavior
(d) negotiation of practices and performances
(e) collective behavior
(f) social influence and group norms
(g) the role of language and communication in forming group identity.[6]

Good leaders will be aware of these processes and know how to effectively address and navigate them amidst cultural differences in the church.

SOCIAL IDENTITY
AND THE OVER-CHURCHED

The over-churched are found in many evangelical churches and help to illustrate these aspects. The over-churched form a subgroup identity within local congregations and are likely to be inoculated from postmodernism and steeped in the Christian subculture as evidenced by interpersonal conflicts, a bent towards legalism, a misunderstanding of separation from the world, an overcommitment to institutionalism, and a fundamental misapprehension of ministry.[7] A more general description is this: a subgroup within many local congregations that has taken the social implications of conversion too far, resulting in missional ineffectiveness. A group like this forms a cultural minority within the larger church setting. The over-churched typically see themselves as a collective, and this confers a social identity. So, even if the leader attempts to build interpersonal relationships, this will help only to the degree that an over-churched person's personal identity is salient. Good leaders don't ignore the communal aspects of congregational life.

A subgroup like the over-churched can create an "us" versus "them" mentality that results in intergroup conflict within the church. This means that members of Christ's body start relating to each other as they would to people outside the faith community. As a result of the characteristics listed above, conflict becomes the norm. Churches that exist in a constant state of conflict are likely wrestling with problems associated with intergroup dynamics.

How can a leader spot this? Do you hear stereotyping occurring? For example, statements like: "the leadership team only cares about getting new people" or "we spend all our money on salaries and not on missions" or "the pastor is ignoring the senior adults in his rush to change the church" or "I just wish they'd sing one hymn on Sunday instead of those Jesus-is-my-boyfriend songs over and over again." These stereotypes directed by the over-churched towards leaders reveal the way the group perceives those in charge. Of course, when pastors hear this type of criticism, fair or not, it usually creates further distance between the groups.

The church setting, however, is technically an intragroup one. That means the tensions evident can be addressed successfully because there is an already-agreed-on shared identity: they are all members of the body of Christ. This suggests that what may be occurring is a type of negotiation. In other words, leaders shouldn't assume the worst but rather the best. Members of this subgroup are at least communicating that the church still matters to them, and that may mean that leaders would actually rather deal with the over-churched than the lack-of-church-commitment folk! The various actions that occur are types of social performances, not inauthentic ones that simply tell the leader where the group is in their thinking. So, complaints about the worship style tell the leadership that the group thinks worship is important. But the complaints also communicate to the leadership team that further teaching on the nature of worship may be needed—or it could be a valid critique that the public worship service has inappropriately accommodated to the culture.

Social influence then is occurring in a mutual way. The subgroup identities are affecting each other, but the key here will be formation of a superordinate or an overarching shared identity. However, the subgroups do not share equal power, because the pastor and elders have the greatest form of social influence: communication. Language is the key to transforming identity, and the preaching and teaching ministry of the church is crucial in this regard. While it can't be developed further here, thinking about preaching and teaching for identity formation offers one way forward in dealing with the over-churched and problems of disunity.

Transformative communication is a dialogue, guided by Scripture and the Spirit, in which social groups within a church develop an awareness of their in-Christ social identity—in the context of their existing personal identities and not to the exclusion of these—in such a way that they begin to live out more fully the social-missional implications of the gospel. Leaders should seek to uncover the various subgroups in their congregation and develop messages that address the underlying issues that influence the groups' beliefs and motivate their actions, rather than focus solely on surface-level issues.[8] Formational communication builds on the following approaches from communication theory: it is (a) dialogical in approach, (b) narrative in structure, (c) communal in orientation, and (d) orthopraxical in theology.

Dialogical communication is an approach that treats teaching and preaching as a conversation. Of course this does not mean that preachers welcome dialogue *during* their sermons. Rather, it means that their sermons begin a larger conversation within the context of the local body. Narrative structure builds on the use of story to bring the scriptural context alive, but it also creates a new or renewed identity as a character to be imitated within the story of the congregation. Communal orientation focuses on the various subgroup identities within a faith community. Finally, orthopraxical ("right practice") theology seeks to restore a balanced relationship between doctrine and practice. These four concepts classify transformative communication, a contextualized approach to teaching and preaching that seeks to form an alternative community with a distinct ethos in comparison to the broader culture, which is also what Paul is doing in 1 Corinthians.[9]

The seven aspects of communal life, listed in the previous section (on page 87), not only adversely affect subgroups like the over-churched, they can also create problems if they are ignored by the church leadership, which should also reflect God-given diversity.[10] Leadership is essential in navigating the challenges of a diverse community. When all the leadership group members share the same social identity, "groupthink" develops. Groupthink operates through "a process of excessive concurrence-seeking that leads members of small cohesive groups to maintain *esprit de corps* by unconsciously developing a number of shared illusions and related norms that interfere with critical thinking and reality testing."[11] Small leadership teams in church settings are highly susceptible to this dynamic. Leaders need to intentionally include diverse voices in the organizational structure of the church. The temptation to follow groupthink is evident in Mark 7:8–9, where tension emerges between God's commands and human traditions. Leaders may believe they are promoting doctrinal unity, rightly seen as essential to Christian identity, while in practice they are imposing a cultural straightjacket on the community, thus working against healthy diversity.

SHARED GROUP BELIEFS
AND SOCIAL IDENTITY

Shared group beliefs are key to the maintenance of social identity. While researchers have uncovered that truth, the passage from 1 John 2 mentioned earlier highlights the centrality of correct teaching for Christian identity. These beliefs have political implications in relation to theology, norms, values, and goals. This is why correct theology is so crucial in ministry. The "condition" necessary for group existence is that "group members have to believe that they constitute a group and/or that they have something in common that united them."[12] So, what should be the central belief around which the body of Christ should gather? The answer is the gospel.

A social identity informed by the gospel resists several identity distortions: (a) I am what I do; (b) I am what has been done to me; and (c) I am my relationships, roles, and responsibilities. Are such aspects of previous identities useful at all? Paul is clear that they are. Describing his own identity in Philippians 3:5, he says he was circumcised, of the people of Israel, the tribe of Benjamin, Hebrew of Hebrews, and a Pharisee. These are all social identities. They are reprioritized in Christ, but they are not erased.

For Paul, the gospel message was foundational to the proclamation of the alternative community with a distinct ethos that he, along with other individuals transformed by God's grace, sought to form in Corinth. A shared group belief in the resurrection was central to the earliest Christ movement (1 Cor. 15:4–8).[13] However, the identity performance of some in Corinth had begun to set this aside: "how can some of you say there is no resurrection of the dead?" (15:12). Shared group beliefs are integral to identity salience. Yet 1 Corinthians 15:12 suggests that a new identity narrative had taken hold in Corinth, one that was not compatible with the gospel discourse they had received (15:1–4). It might have come out of Roman and Jewish contexts that had no room for belief in the resurrection. Or, this identity narrative without the resurrection could have resulted from Paul's earlier focus on the cross as central (2:2).[14] Either way, the categories that governed the thinking of the Corinthian Christ followers did not match those that Paul wanted them to develop.

If the problem was that the Corinthians continued to claim participation in the Christ-following community while behaving according to Corinthian and/or Greco-Roman norms, that would explain why Paul quotes a Corinthian slogan and a Greek play (15:32–33). There seems to be confusion over the way existing identities are reprioritized in Christ (7:18; 10:31; 12:2). These identity dilemmas—where the Corinthians' identity in Christ intersected their civic and cultural identities—are evident all throughout 1 Corinthians. More specifically, it seems that existing social identifications were negating shared group beliefs, such as belief in the resurrection, that were essential to the gospel tradition.[15]

Gospel identity is a result not only of shared group beliefs, but also of God's work. After describing Christ's appearance to him and his persecution of the earliest Jesus followers, Paul writes, "By the grace of God I am what I am" (1 Cor. 15:10). He highlights his sense of personal identity, the way he differs from other Christ followers. It's not that others have not received God's grace. But for Paul, this gift of grace gives him his sense of mission and the focus for who he is and what he does. Even though this sounds like an individual identity, it is still an issue of group belonging. Paul is part of a network of others involved in the gentile mission (16:5–12), and the context of 15:8–11 highlights the interpersonal and intergroup continuum that is crucial to social identity. Furthermore, although his self-categorization as an "apostle" seems to be contested by others, he still ends the list of witnesses with himself (9:1–3; 15:8–10). In fact, it is because of Paul's previous persecution of the movement that he has come to understand the nature of God's grace. After this interpersonal digression, he brings other leaders and himself together in an inclusive "we," reminding the Corinthians that Christ's resurrection is central to the gospel of grace, a message the leaders "proclaim" and which the Corinthians had "come to believe" (15:11 NRSV).

As mentioned above, belief in the resurrection is integral to a gospel identity. With his argument in 1 Corinthians 15:12–19, Paul is ensuring the coherence of the group. Social identity is formed through categorization of ingroups and outgroups, but that is not the only factor. Shared group beliefs provide a basis for the ongoing existence of the group. For Paul, without a belief in the resurrection of Christ and its accompanying hope in their own resurrection through God's grace, there is no reason for Christ groups to continue in the faith. Thus, in chapter 15, he goes to great length to remind them of the gospel tradition he had previously passed on to them.

For Paul, communicating group norms based on the gospel drove much of what he wrote in 1 Corinthians. Upholding the church's unity in our contemporary context requires a similar communication strategy. Effective leaders deploy scriptural-based and research-based tools as they navigate the crossroads of the gospel and culture. The difficulties associated with today's cultural context are not unique. Christians in Nazi Germany wrestled with similar issues when their Christian and cultural identities were, or should have been, at odds. As we unpack these tools, we will learn from the example of the White Rose Society, a student-led leaflet distribution movement from the University of Munich that rose to the occasion to face the evil of their day through the power of the gospel.

SOCIAL IDENTITY, ROLES, AND HIERARCHIES

The roles we play are key contributors to understanding our social identity. They govern our attitudes, behaviors, and relationships. If you were to answer the question "Who am I?" your responses would probably center on your roles. The focus here is not so much on your individual differences but the way societal expectations impact your behavior. The commitments you make reflect your prior determination of the importance of these roles—or even the rejection of those imposed roles.

The White Rose Society is an example of this role negotiation. Sophie Scholl and her brother Hans were part of a student movement that distributed leaflets protesting the Nazi regime. They eventually gave their lives for their beliefs. When asked why they would do such a thing, they replied, "We are Christian, and we are German, therefore we are responsible for Germany."[16] Their sense of who they were and where they were pushed them to resist the evil in their world.

Identity performances are the activities of an individual

that occur in the presence of a group. They are part of a process of negotiation with others in which people think of themselves from the perspective of others. An identity is thought to be prominent when it reflects the priorities and behaviors that would be acceptable to the group in the moment. This doesn't mean that other identities are irrelevant; they are simply lower down the priority list and not acted upon—though they may still serve as a secondary influence. This also means that there are dis-identifications, groups or roles that are rejected. These oppositions reveal key insights about a person.

Hans Scholl's initial motivation to oppose the Nazi regime came from hearing a sermon on the moral injustices that were occurring. He and Sophie distributed leaflets among other students at the University of Munich, some of whom were influenced by professors who were critical of the regime. Hans drew on Goethe and Schiller, two German literary giants, for quotations in his writing and presentations. This would have encouraged his literarily informed readers to go to Goethe or Schiller to see the context, which then would have made more explicit what he was calling his German compatriots to do. The combination of political, literary, and theological allusions combined to produce persuasive leaflets. Hans, however, would later write about the constant temptation he felt to give up on their mission: "I'm weak and I'm puny but I want to do what is right."[17]

Identity and behavior are based on a shared set of meanings. If one can discern a person's identity, then it is likely one can anticipate his or her behavior. This is not just about internal thinking processes; it is also about the social structure. The Scholls had an already-internalized Christian identity that was activated in light of the political setting in Germany. The cultural setting allowed Hans to draw new insights and applications from his reading of Augustine that propelled him and the other members of the Society into action. One key way to understand these domains is the identity hierarchy, in which superordinate and subgroup identities might exist in a nested way. The identity hierarchy allows identities to be organized in various situations in a way that certain behaviors can be encouraged and others discouraged, which then results in a situationally specific social identification. In order to organize these aspects of a person's life, one must focus on the idea of a master identity. This is an overarching or superordinate identity that informs all the other subgroup ones. For the Scholls, their master or superordinate identity was their Christian identity. This wasn't simply an abstract theological one. It was one that had to be embodied in the context of their German identity, and that was the challenge, of course.

Hans wrote in his diary: "My pessimism gets worse every day. Skepticism is poisoning my soul."[18] He struggled with what to do. The challenge for Hans, as for us, is to live in such a way that our social identity becomes consistent with our personal identity, both of which are sourced in who we are in Christ as members of the body of Christ.

There are several positive benefits to having multiple identities. When a person willingly embodies an identity, it provides guidance for behavior and increases a person's cognitive awareness. However, when others impose those same identities, the benefits do not accrue in the same way. Some have found the imagery of a computer network and its various nodes, or points of entry, as a good way to describe the way multiple identities work. Information doesn't flow just one way.

Context and other inputs, such as the Bible, mutually interpret one another to form meaning for the person. Obviously, not everyone will experience multiple identities to the same degree. High-status and wealthy people tend to have more of these than low-status and poor ones. Sophie's Christian identity was informed less through intellectual efforts and more through digging into the Bible to understand what she should do amid the injustice around her. Hans's growth was nurtured by his books and his interactions with theologian Carl Muth, the editor of the banned journal *Hochland*. Their identities as Christians, Germans, students, and siblings functioned differently throughout their experiences in the German nightmare, but as Steven Garber recalls concerning Sophie and Hans, "Brother and sister began to find a place to stand. Reading the Scriptures in light of the challenge presented in their culture, having conversations with friends about the world and their place in it, meeting older, wiser people who offered them their time and their books—together they molded a vision about what was real and true and right."[19] Their conclusion in light of the negotiation of their existing identities: "We are responsible for Germany!"

Let's return to 1 Corinthians in order to see how thinking about social identity sheds light on what's going on in that letter. Paul negotiates and transforms existing social identities of the Corinthians in order to extend his mission. Like some of the over-churched today, some of the Corinthians had misunderstood the nature of separation from the world (1 Cor. 5:9–11) and misapprehended the nature of ministry (1 Cor. 3:5–17). Paul's solution is not to retreat from the culture but to engage it through mission as social identification (1 Cor. 10:31—11:1; 14:23). This approach sees existing identities as crucial for effective mission, since an abandonment of these would result in missional ineffectiveness.[20]

THREE CASE STUDIES
OF SOCIAL IDENTITY IN 1 CORINTHIANS

1 Corinthians 7:17–24:
Superordinate and Subgroup Identities

Paul's "rule in all the churches" is that Christians are to live according to the call of God (7:17). The NRSV translation—"let each of you lead the life that the Lord has assigned, to which God has called you"—gives the impression that Paul has a state or vocation in mind, and some interpreters have concluded that Paul rejects all social or legal status changes or identity transformations for followers of Christ. Part of the problem is that interpreters often think the words *assigned* and *called* are near synonyms. And because 7:20–24 also discusses "call," they bring the meaning of *assigned* into these verses as well. However, the two terms refer to different aspects of the Christians' identity. The first, *assigned*, refers to all the various life practices that result from different spiritual gifts. (Similarly, the "gift" in 7:7 results in a different manner of life [see also Rom. 12:3].) The second, *called*, as it is used in 7:17, 20, and 21, is an interior call to be in Christ. Paul's "rule" concerns *who* people consider themselves to be. For Paul, being in Christ is the master identity that realigns all other aspects of one's life. However, some of the Corinthians were giving up this new identity in Christ when they prioritized key aspects of their Roman social identity. This indicates that Paul's earliest opposition came mostly from those who saw that his gospel would get in the way of the kinship, loyalty, economic, gender, and social patterns already in place. In such situations, the pressure not to remain in their calling with God must have been intense.[21]

Calling does not erase all other identities, yet it does reorient social life. Ethnic identity indexes such as "circumcision" and "uncircumcision" do not disappear, but their importance is reprioritized (7:18). Thus, Paul teaches the community to continue to identify with the ethnic group they belonged to when they began to follow Christ. Both Jewish and non-Jewish ethnic identities continue as valid expressions of life in Christ. This is a particularistic approach to Christ-movement social identity (10:32). Paul doesn't ask the community to stop the practices that fit their respective ethnic identities. He simply reminds them that obeying God's commands must come first (7:19; Gal. 5:6; 6:15).

The NRSV continues, "Let each of you remain in the condition in which you were called" (7:20). The Greek word underlying the English word "condition" would be better translated as "calling." The calling in view here is the call of God through Christ to be in Christ. This verse, then, does not sanctify the social status quo nor suggest that a person is called to be a slave or to remain as one. Paul is saying Christians should remain in the calling in Christ into which they were called. Thus, there is no social situation too dire that would hinder a person from responding positively through the Spirit to God's call. A slave working in a copper mine in Greece can respond to God's call just as a Roman woman whose husband continues to honor his provincial deities. Paul does not diminish the challenges associated with such responses. His point is God's call transcends even those conditions. While our contemporary context differs from Paul's, today these might include: an incarcerated individual, a person in extreme poverty, a person whose spouse rejects Christianity, or a Pakistani migrant on the island of Lesbos, Greece. The gospel call reaches past even the most difficult circumstances. No one is excluded from God's family.

In 7:21, Paul is concerned about the social implications of the gospel for slaves. Bartchy's translation is helpful: "Were you a slave when you were called? Don't worry about it. But if, indeed, you become manumitted, by all means [as a freedman/woman] live according to God's calling."[22] His point here is that even if you can gain your freedom and thus a new social status, it is still God's call that ultimately defines your identity. This idea is central to Paul's instructions concerning marriage and celibacy throughout 1 Corinthians 7. In earlier passages, Paul challenged aspects of Roman social life that were getting in the way of the salience of an in-Christ social identity. Now he addresses an aspect of Roman social life that some thought could adversely affect one's relationship with God: slavery. Paul transforms the social stigma of slavery so that it becomes an index, metaphorical or otherwise, of an in-Christ identity within the Christ movement (7:22–23). All Christians, therefore, even those with differences that remain, should be accepted because all share the same interior call. Paul concludes his discussion with the reminder: in "whatever" calling "you were called, brothers and sisters, there remain with God" (7:24).

1 Corinthians 9:19–23: Mission as Social Identification with Jews and Gentiles

J. Hudson Taylor was well known for identifying socially with those to whom he was called. Missiologist Marvin Newell writes, "Taylor, a pioneer missionary to China, was known for his sensitivity to Chinese culture and dress. For example, he wore Chinese clothing, which was rare for Westerners at that time, and even wore the customary pigtail with shaven forehead."[23] During this period, other missionaries sought to bring British culture to China. Yet Taylor saw the importance of maintaining China's indigenous culture in the context of his gospel mission.

Similarly, one of Paul's solutions to the problems of food offered to idols and civic engagements is mission as social identification. Paul writes in 9:19 (NRSV) that he is "free with respect to all." Yet he has also "made" himself "a slave to all." He acts in this way to "win more of them." Too often, this verse is understood to mean Paul thinks he is free from the constraints of Israel's scriptural tradition. But the freedom in view here is, on one hand, from becoming indebted to human masters and, on the other, from prioritizing his own safety or advantage in his interactions with others. This freedom in turn allows him to serve others as their apostle, as one who willingly gives up certain rights for his mission among the nations.

Paul then in 9:20–21 addresses his continuing social identification with those who are part of his ethnic group: "To the Jews I became as a Jew, in order to win Jews." The presence of "as" suggests to many interpreters that Paul had ceased to be a Jew, or that he identified himself as such only in certain missionary situations. However, it is more likely that this refers to Paul's variety of practices as he relates to Diaspora ethnic Jews generally, especially in the areas of hospitality and table fellowship, which is part of the larger context of 8:1–11:1. Paul then describes another group: "those under the law." If this simply refers to the Jews, it would be redundant. So Paul probably has something else in view. It is quite likely that "under the law" refers to a subgroup identity, a group following a stricter interpretation of the Scriptures, possibly associated with the Pharisees. Paul's past as a Pharisee (Phil. 3:5) would allow him to follow Pharisaic guidelines to reach this group with the gospel, even though he is "not under the law"—meaning the strict interpretations of this group.

The next group Paul brings up is "those outside the law." This reference to gentiles emphasizes their sinfulness (9:21; Gal. 2:15). In discussing his approach to this group, Paul notes that he is "not free from God's law" but is "under Christ's law." In light of 7:17–20, where Jews in Christ are called to live as Jews, one might expect that Paul would follow his own "rule" (7:17). Yet the phrase "Christ's law" has vexed interpreters. David Rudolph suggests that it *"refers to God's law (the law of Moses) in the hand of Christ as reflected in Christ's association with sinners."*[24] This interpretation fits well with Paul's hope to "win those outside the law." This word for "win" here is used five times in 9:19–22, suggesting that the crucial point here is mission. The Pharisees, in fact, used this term for "recruiting new members through table-fellowship and living among the masses."[25] This interpretation becomes even more likely when we consider the description of a Pharisaic mission in Matthew 23:15 with Paul's personal history in Philippians 3:8.

Paul's mission of social identification is further described in 9:22–23, when he writes, "To the weak I became weak, so that I might win the weak." The term "weak" is often thought to refer to those who are not in Christ. This would make sense in light of 9:23, where Paul says he does all of this "for the sake of the gospel." However, Paul's work of identity construal is broader than a one-time experience (1:18; see also Phil. 2:12). In the present context, "weak" refers to a subgroup identity within the Christ movement in Corinth for whom eating food offered to idols had "become a stumbling block" (8:7, 9). If the earlier discussion concerning "win" is considered, especially in light of Matthew 18:15, then broader aspects of identity formation are part of Paul's "gospel" mission. This subgroup may instead be those who were poor and disadvantaged, and therefore more impacted by eating restrictions. They could easily have been termed "weak" in light of Roman cultural expectations of strength (1:26–29). Paul identifies socially with this group by working "with [his] own hands" as a "tentmaker" in Corinth and by refusing to participate in Roman patronage (4:10, 12; see also Acts 18:3, 11, 18). It is likely that social identification with others is part of the imitation that Paul had in mind as he instructs the Corinthians to follow him as he follows Christ (11:1; 2 Cor. 6:10; 8:9; Luke 4:13–14, 21).

1 Corinthians 16:1–4:
The Formation of an Economic Identity

A transformed group ethos emerges in new economic practices, since economic decisions are ones of identity. In 16:1–4, Paul seeks to form the economic aspects of the Corinthians' in-Christ social identity by instructing them "concerning the collection for the saints." This is generally known as the Jerusalem collection (see Rom. 15:26; 2 Cor. 8:13–15; Gal. 2:10). Paul offers different reasons for the collection based on the rhetorical context of each of these letters, but one aspect is consistent: he connects gentiles in Christ to God's covenant people, Israel. This passage in 1 Corinthians is one of Paul's earliest references to the collection and is also another example of the "now concerning" formula, which suggests this issue was raised previously by the Corinthians themselves. Perhaps they were asking for clarification on the details of the project, or more likely some were interested in giving to the collection as a benefaction.[26] In the latter case, they would give to help Christians in Jerusalem and then expect that those in Jerusalem would, in turn, return honor and allegiance to them. In this way, an existing identity related to patronage contributed to the deformation of an in-Christ social identity among the Corinthians.

Paul uses the term "the collection" in 16:1–2. This term generally referred to business documents such as tax reports or money intended for pagan worship rituals—like the collection of Isis. Notably, this is the only place where Paul uses this word. Elsewhere, he describes his financial project as "the service" (2 Cor. 9:1) or "the participation" (2 Cor. 8:4), which both seem more in keeping with Paul's perspective on life within the body of Christ. His use of "the collection" suggests that the Corinthians may have misunderstood what it was because of their socially and culturally influenced thinking about patronage. Paul, on the other hand, emphasizes mutuality and relationality. Further, since such collections were made to Isis, some of the Corinthians may have thought of Paul's collection as a type of benefaction directed to a provincial deity, a view equally problematic for Paul (12:2). In general, Paul works to transform their thinking regarding patronage, which he likely refers to in 16:3 when he describes "your gift to Jerusalem," since the Greek word underlying "gift" is taken from the patronage context. For Paul, God's "gift" transforms these one-way-oriented approaches into expressions of mutuality and economic flourishing marked by generosity. The Corinthians' participation will reveal the degree to which their in-Christ identity is salient, and a later epistle suggests they eventually did contribute (see Rom. 15:26).

Dobie Gray's song "The In Crowd" offered little hope to those members not in the in crowd. The gospel, however, does offer hope and calls us to embrace those outside our ingroup. Leroy Barber, cofounder of The Voices Project, lists some of those we might seek to avoid: "Those you just don't click with; the disagreeable; the folks beneath you; control freaks; liars and backstabbers; or criminals."[27] We often want to avoid these types of people, but "we are called to a different perspective, a perspective that challenges us to embrace others instead of create boundaries. As followers of Christ, the perspective of embrace matters most."[28] We are called to the uncomfortableness of outgroup mission. We follow the example of Jesus in the healing of the centurion's servant (Matt. 8:5–13) and the Canaanite woman's daughter (Matt. 15:21–28). God's work will often be found among the outgroups of our culture.

So what can we learn from these three case studies as we seek to apply them within the context of the local church? First, in light of 7:17–24, leaders should take seriously the idea that diverse patterns of life may not be simply a contemporary identity project but rather a matter of calling. This suggests further that leaders need to recognize that diverse patterns of life are not something to be removed from the local church. Instead, these patterns are to be expected, as they were evident among the earliest followers of Christ. Wise leaders should resist the temptation to eliminate diverse expressions of life.

Second, Paul's model in 9:19–23 provides another reason for maintaining diverse patterns of life: mission as social identification. Existing identities are not an end in and of themselves but are to serve as vehicles for advancing the gospel among those in our social orbit. Wise leaders encourage social integration rather than isolation. The social life of Christians should be a positive factor in the salvation of their friends and family members.

Third, in light of 16:1–4, ministry leaders must take seriously the formation of church attendees' economic identity. This means encouraging them to promote the gospel financially and to develop generosity. Early Christianity played a significant role in providing care for those hurting within the Roman empire. Church leaders need to help cultivate that same mindset and practice in their congregations today, rather than leave their people assuming care is a responsibility only for government agencies.

Finally, leaders should aim to close the gap between Sunday morning and Monday morning. Too often, those in the business world, for example, think the church has little to offer in relation to their work life. Thus, developing a sermon series or small-group studies on vocation, work, and economic flourishing might prove helpful. Paying close attention to existing social identities will help reveal ministry gaps that need attention and provide a way to support the unity of the church amidst diversity.

Questions for Reflection

1. What are the top three group memberships that
   you value most, and why are they important
   to you?
2. What sort of groups do you find in your church?
   Do any of them cause problems? If so, why?
3. What do you think about Paul's rule that people
   should continue to identify with their existing
   ethnic identity even while following Christ
   (1 Cor. 7:17–24)? Why do you think he considered
   this important?
4. Paul changed his behavior based on changing
   contexts and differing identities of those present
   (1 Cor. 9:19-23). What would it mean for you to
   adjust to another person's identity for the purpose
   of mission?

5

ONE
AMONG MANY

Have you ever "unfollowed" one of your Christian friends on Facebook because you couldn't handle their political views? Or maybe you received criticism because of who you voted for in the last election. Have you ever found yourself longing for the good old days in the worship service when the songs were recognizable and the volume was bearable? Do they really *have* to sing the same choruses over and again? Or can you recall a situation when you felt uncomfortable with "those kind of people" when you noticed them in a church service, people different from you in some significant way? Perhaps you thought they would be more comfortable in a service that was designed for their own kind. Politics, worship styles, and personal biases are just some of the challenges church folk face as they try to navigate their personal identity along with their membership in the body of Christ.

The lens that the Bible uses to help us understand ourselves is both individual and collective. The church is one body made of many members (1 Cor. 12:27). We cannot see ourselves as mere individuals. Yet we do not lose our individual identity in Christ (1 Cor. 7:18–20). In the New Testament, the designation "temple of the Holy Spirit" (1 Cor. 6:19 ESV) is ascribed both to the individual believer and the entire faith community. The church is a collective by nature. The bond that knits individual believers together is spiritual. We are joined to one another because we are united with Christ. Unfortunately, this spiritual reality does not guarantee either a cohesive culture or a community that expresses mutual concern for its individual members.

It's no accident that the epistle that speaks most clearly of our identity as one among many was addressed to the sharply divided church in Corinth. It alerts us to the pitfalls we face in wrestling with our identity. Some in Corinth overidentified with their leaders in a way that set them against others. They even identified themselves with Christ in a way that set them against other members of Christ's body. In order to have a biblically shaped identity, we must learn to hold our individual identity in balance with our corporate identity. And Paul shows us a way to do this in his letter to Philemon. We must know when to subordinate the particularities of our individual sense of self to our collective identity as part of the body of Christ.

DIVISIONS IN THE BODY IN CORINTH

One of the many problems the Corinthian church wrestled with was an overidentification with their Roman social identity. We see this unhealthy tendency in many of their actions. They were dividing around key personalities (1 Cor. 1:12). They over-relied on the world's wisdom (1 Cor. 2:5). They had an inordinate trust in Roman officials (1 Cor. 2:6–9). They had a misplaced confidence in Roman law courts, which were central in enforcing Roman identity (1 Cor. 6:1–11). And their social hierarchy relied on patronage relationships, the primary economic model in antiquity (1 Cor. 3:3–4; 4:8; 11:17–34). Civic identity had become a problem for the congregation, which resulted in "divisions" within the body (1 Cor. 11:18). This was so much the case that Paul had to ask, "Is Christ divided?" (1 Cor. 1:13).

We see Paul's goal for the community in 1 Corinthians 1:10: "I appeal to you, brothers and sisters, in the name of our Lord Jesus Christ, that all of you agree with one another in what you say and that there be no divisions among you, but that you be perfectly united in mind and thought." To accomplish this, Paul addresses issues related to identity in chapters 1–4, and then he instructs the Corinthians on issues related to individual ethics in chapters 5–10. In chapters 11–16, he offers guidance in the formation of the group's ethos. Paul recognized that identity influences individual ethics, which when expressed in a group setting also produce a group ethos. Leaders seeking to maintain or restore unity in a church need to sustain a balanced focus on these three areas: identity, ethics, and ethos.

Paul focuses on the transformation of the group ethos in the last part of the letter, and after addressing issues related to worship practices, he writes, "Just as a body, though one, has many parts, but all its many parts form one body, so it is with Christ" (1 Cor. 12:12). This may be another example of Corinthian Roman social identity causing problems in the church. The imagery of a group of people as a body was well-known in Roman politics. Menenius Agrippa used it to reestablish a hierarchical relationship between the senate and the plebeians. His point was that each segment of society had a role to play and should remain in their social stations for the common good. His purpose was to maintain the existing order for the ruling elites and to tell the masses they had no choice but to submit to this order.[1]

In light of the problems in Corinth associated with Roman political identity, it's likely that just such a status-based approach to communal life had taken root in the church, especially when one considers the mistreatment of the poor at the Lord's Supper (1 Cor. 11:17–34). Paul, as an intercultural mediator, took this well-known imagery and reused it to point out the way status reversals are the norm within the church. Those who were undesirables among the Romans were given honor in the "body" (1 Cor. 12:22–24). It is likely that the problems associated with tongues were also linked to social stratification (1 Cor. 14:18–20). Paul identified with the higher-status group initially but then switched to offer a transformed approach to worship. "In declaring this," Kar Lim explains, "Paul is also instructing those who perceived that they might have higher social status because of the possession of the gift of tongues to give up their rights to speak for the sake of the weaker brother so that there would be no schism in the body (1 Cor. 12:25)."[2] By doing this, Paul is marking identity boundaries for the group and noting that they are different than the status-based ones evident in the broader culture. The identity of the group as the body of Christ is made evident through the inclusion of the weak and poor, those the broader culture would set aside as deplorable.

IDENTIFICATION WITH CHRIST

Paul emphasized the close connection between Christ and those who claim to follow Him. This may harken to his experience on the Damascus road where the risen Christ associated the members of the church with Himself (Acts 9:1–5). Identification with Christ refers to the position every believer has in Jesus on the basis of His work and the appropriation of it by the individual believer's faith. This is accomplished by the Holy Spirit as an act of divine grace. Paul describes it in 1 Corinthians 12:13 when he writes, "For we were all baptized by one Spirit so as to form one body—whether Jews or Gentiles, slave or free—and we were all given the one Spirit to drink." And in Galatians 3:27, he describes this experience as being "baptized into Christ."

We are united with Christ (John 15:1–6; Gal. 2:20; Eph. 2:6). Scripture's teaching on our union with Christ is crucial for the formation of a salient identity. Theologian J. Todd Billings describes it this way: "Union with Christ . . . entails the giving of a new identity such that in Christ, forgiveness and new life are received through the Spirit. Union with Christ involves abiding in Christ the Vine. It means that through the Spirit, sinners are adopted in the household of God as co-heirs with Christ."[3] Those who are in Christ have at their disposal the cognitive, evaluative, and emotional resources to overcome a life of failure, guilt, and frustration—both personally and with others (1 Cor. 2:10–16).

The last phrase, "with others," is especially important. Union with Christ is not just a personal doctrine. It is also a social one. As a result of being united to Christ the Head, all individual believers—members of Christ's body—are united to each other. Naomi Ellemers recognizes that the three components mentioned above (cognitive, evaluative, and emotional) contribute to a sense of social identity: "a *cognitive* component (a cognitive awareness of one's membership in a social group—self-categorization), an *evaluative* component (a positive or negative value connotation attached to this group membership—group self-esteem), and an *emotional* component (a sense of emotional involvement with the group—affective commitment)."[4] These three components are important to keep in mind as we seek to uphold the unity of the church while maintaining and honoring our respective differences. Too often, union with Christ is seen only as a theological point and not a social one. It is more than a point of belief. It is also a way of life.

Seeing union with Christ only as a doctrine often results in the fossilization of Christian identity. Fossilization occurs when theological constructs designed to address earlier cultural settings are transported to a different era without proper contextualization. The way to overcome fossilization is to translate union with Christ in a way that retains its essential content while restating it in contemporary terms. Union with Christ doesn't require only one way of living. Christian identity adapts to various cultural circumstances. William S. Campbell notes that in-Christ language is metaphorical.[5] But on what basis is the believer's being in Christ or in union with Christ construed as a metaphor rather than a reality? Being in Christ is conceptual (lending coherence to Paul's writing) and also contributes to shaping these new realities based on existing ways of acting, knowing, and communicating. In this way, in Christ becomes a "metaphor we live by."[6]

Union with Christ contributes to the formation of both a personal and social identity and does so in ways that allow for diverse expressions of these formations in a new, transformed common identity. It allows church attendees to stop thinking in an "us" versus "them" way, since it opens up a realization of a new, other group with which we should identify. This could be described as a "superordinate" identity, a larger group identity that transcends our smaller identities. This way of thinking can help reduce conflict. When "they" become "we" in the body of Christ, Cleveland notes, at least four changes occur: "we naturally like them a whole lot more; we're more open to receiving helpful criticism from them; we forgive them more easily and are less likely to expect them to experience collective guilt; and we treat each other better."[7]

I (Brian) saw this occur when several students approached one of our staff members concerning the type of language that was used in an illustration. The middle-aged leader wasn't aware that his description was perceived as sexist to many of the younger generation. As the group sat together and discussed the different cultural settings they were raised in, a mutual understanding and empathy was expressed. The conversation ended with the group developing a newfound awareness of their differences and an appreciation for what they have in common: their common in-Christ identity and shared passion to reach others with the gospel. Through this interaction, the staff member learned to think about his language and illustrations while the students developed an appreciation for the cultural baggage older leaders sometimes have to navigate and overcome to reach a new generation with the gospel. In this case, the "they" became "we," and it allowed for more effective ministry to occur.

Obviously, these changes would go a long way in reducing church-based conflicts. Union with Christ is at the same time union with other Christians. The work of the Spirit knits disparate individuals into one body (Eph. 2:22; 1 Peter 2:4–5) and calls Christians to live out who they already are in Christ. For this reason, Paul's admonitions in Romans 6:1–14 are structured around the indicatives of Christian identity—you are in Christ (Rom. 6:1–10)—and the imperatives that follow from that identity—now live like it (Rom. 6:11–14). The believer's old life has been crucified with Christ, and a new one has resulted—one that is free from the power of sin. But Paul's teaching about one's union with Christ in Romans 6:3–10 is about breaking the power of sin, not about erasing previously existing identity-based differences.

THE INDIVIDUAL
AND THE COMMUNITY TOGETHER

The individual and the community belong together in Paul's theology. The apostle does not conceive of a solitary individual. In 1 Corinthians 12:27, he writes, "Now you are the body of Christ and individually members of it" (ESV). For Paul, identity is derived from being a member of Christ's body.[8] This is important for us as North Americans, since we generally tend to think of ourselves as individuals first. It is vital that we not downplay or even overemphasize either the individual or the communal. Rather, we need to keep both of these identities in balance, otherwise we'll miss foundational aspects of Paul's theology. For Paul, the Christian is an individual in community, one who lives by the principle of unity amid diversity. As a result, each member has a team mindset in which the group is capable of accomplishing more than would otherwise be possible for the individual.

In the final race scene in the movie *Seabiscuit*, the horse's jockey, Red, reflects on the way the team originally saw its role to shape Seabiscuit into a winner. But he says in the end, "Seabiscuit fixed us." The shared mission and goal between the trainer, owner, and jockey resulted in mutual support that transformed each individual in needed ways. Seabiscuit couldn't win without them, and they couldn't have moved beyond their brokenness without each other. The trainer, owner, and jockey maintained their unique identities and roles, but their shared life and goal allowed them to accomplish more together than each could have alone.

The local congregation is not just *compared* to the body; it *is* the body of Christ. The whole is greater than the sum of its parts, just as Seabiscuit, Red, and the team were. The imagery in 1 Corinthians 12 reveals a close connection between Christ and the church. In 3:23, Paul claims that the church has a Christ-defined identity. As we discovered in chapter 4, individual identities are not obliterated but are transformed through union with Christ. This means members of Christ's body have dual identities: one that is communal and one that is individual. Paul says as much in 12:27: "Now you are the body of Christ, and each one of you is a part of it."

A leader, for example, can shift the attention of the congregation to the identity that the church members seem to be neglecting and that is causing division (small group, gender, ethnic, individual, corporate, denominational, etc.). By acknowledging one overemphasized identity and reprioritizing it in reference to a higher one (that is, one's in-Christ identity), a pastor could preach a sermon that is likely to motivate church members to expend more effort in living out the highlighted identity. This insight will be crucial in helping congregational leaders uphold the church's unity while maintaining each person's uniqueness.

Consider the tension between small-group ministry and congregational worship celebration. Often leaders who have seen church fights in the past view small groups as breeding grounds for cliques or settings for people to complain about the church's leadership. The solution isn't to get rid of small-group ministry, but rather to help the congregation see the need for a balance between the small group and the larger celebrations. Healthy congregations maintain both. Those who emphasize the importance of community building that occurs in the small-group setting are correct but miss the important unifying factor that occurs during corporate worship. Those who dismiss the value of small groups significantly overlook the need for accountability and community that can occur only in those intimate settings. A social identity approach to pastoral leadership would discern which side is being overemphasized and help the congregation reprioritize it in relation to the underemphasized value.

Having to reprioritize values is not just a challenge we face today. Paul had to wrestle with such a challenge as he sought to reconcile an early church leader named Philemon and his slave, Onesimus.

N. T. Wright has called that small letter to Philemon a perfect snapshot of Paul's theology.[9] All of the detailed argumentation that is evident in his other letters is distilled down in this most personal communication. Philemon provides a good example of the way this individual-communal identity was addressed in Paul's day. It also offers wisdom for maintaining unity amid continuing differences in the church. Timothy Keller has observed that "those who have been given a Christian identity have the resources to become more open to difference and to become more culturally flexible than they would ever have been otherwise."[10] Being open to difference and the ability to be culturally flexible are two of the most important ways we maintain church unity amid our individual uniqueness. In Philemon, Paul demonstrates these characteristics in surprisingly helpful ways.

PAUL, PHILEMON, AND ONESIMUS IN THE BODY OF CHRIST

Paul's statements about Christian unity in Galatians 3:28, 1 Corinthians 12:13, and Colossians 3:11 could sound as if no existing social identity is relevant in Christ and that Christ-following slaves should no longer be identified as such. Two main interpretive approaches have tried to determine the social implications of these verses: the universalistic and the particularistic. The universalistic approach contends that in Christ, existing social distinctions lose their relevance or are in some sense erased. The particularistic approach argues that these identities are reprioritized in Christ but can and do continue to remain situationally salient. In Philemon, we see the "slave or free" issue clearly, and thinking about the way Paul navigates this may help us address some of the complexities associated with socioeconomic distinctions in the church today.

What's going on in this letter? Various reconstructions have been proposed regarding the context of the letter to Philemon. The first approach describes Onesimus as a runaway slave. Another view, the friend of the master approach, does not see Onesimus as a fugitive but as one who intended to return to his master's household once he had received a promise of intercession from his owner's friend (Paul). In a third view, Onesimus is believed to have been sent by the church to provide Paul with aid while in prison. While each of these views has limitations and while the brief nature of the letter does not provide further clarity, paying attention to the group dynamics may give us insight as to what's really going on. Paul's letter, in turn, can help us see how social identity continues to be a factor in relationships within the church.

In Philemon, several different social groups are mentioned. We find one group in v. 2: the congregation that meets in Philemon's house. The members of this house assembly are described as the saints (vv. 5, 7 ESV). Thus, church and the saints may have functioned to reinforce the unity of all the Christ followers, since they emphasize an overarching social identity for the group.

Paul describes another social group through the use of "brother." He uses it for the letter's co-sender, Timothy, "our brother" (v. 1). He uses the term for Philemon (vv. 7 and 20) and for Onesimus, with a significant increase in emotion—a "beloved brother" (v. 16 ESV). It is likely that "brothers" functioned as a widespread term describing members of the Christ movement as a new kinship group.

In Philemon, Paul seems to be emphasizing the way these individuals now embody a shared ingroup prototype—that is, the way they embody what the group values. Philemon and

Onesimus are now both brothers in Christ, but what should be done when a Christ-following slave owner has a slave who is also a member of the Christ movement? This was a significant challenge for the earliest Christians who sought to understand the social implications of the gospel and what it means to be one among many in the body. Our challenges today are different, but Paul's approach may prove helpful for us church leaders as we navigate overlapping relational networks in the church.

Paul as an Entrepreneur of Onesimus's Dual Identities

Paul, acting as an "entrepreneur" of identity, offers guidelines for defining and maintaining identity within the church. In this letter, he uses a process that social identity theory describes as "recategorization." This, as a leadership approach, will shift thinking from "us" and "them" to a more inclusive "we."[11] Paul does this first by recategorizing Onesimus. While he is still a slave and a debtor, he is also Paul's "child," "heart," and "brother" (vv. 10, 12, 16 ESV).

Philemon is likewise recategorized by Paul in relation to Onesimus. He is now Philemon's "brother" (v. 16). To emphasize the positive nature of this renewed interdependence, Paul reminds Philemon of the nature of their own relationship: he is Paul's "fellow worker," "brother," "partner," and debtor (vv. 1, 7, 17, 19b). Paul's language highlights the reciprocal nature of the relationship between the three of them while emphasizing the renewed kinship that should reduce hostility and increase cooperation in the Pauline mission, the social project in view in this letter (vv. 11, 13, 17).

Several key ideas can help reduce conflict and increase the

likelihood of intergroup cooperation: a common fate, positive interdependence, and a common identity. All three are expressed in this letter.

Common fate is evident in Paul's desire for the three men to work together. He characterizes Philemon as a leader of a house assembly and a "fellow worker" in the Pauline movement (vv. 1–2). He is also described as Paul's partner and debtor (vv. 17–19b). Into this relationship of positive interdependence, Paul inserts Onesimus as one who now can be an integral part of the continuation and expansion of the gentile mission in Asia Minor, an apt description of their shared superordinate goal (vv. 6, 11, 13). A common identity must precede, and in fact, produces, positive interdependence.[12] By this point, it's clear that Paul, Philemon, and Onesimus share a common identity as members of Christ's body (vv. 10, 16).

This construction of a superordinate identity does not eliminate or obliterate existing subgroup identities. The universalistic approach runs the risk of elevating the dominant culture and giving cultural norms a theological significance they do not deserve. The key to conflict resolution is to recognize the dual nature of group identity. According to Haslam, "The key to satisfactory conflict resolution lies not in increasing the salience of [superordinate] social identity *at the expense of* subgroup identity (that is, recategorization . . .) but in acknowledging and allowing expression of both superordinate *and* subgroup identities."[13] This dual identity recognizes the continued importance of subgroup identities in the formation of superordinate social identity salience. The combination of the two kinds of identity increases the likelihood of group goal achievement.

This approach was used in a study that tried to resolve

tensions between loggers and environmentalists regarding the cutting down of trees in the Pacific Northwest. What the negotiators discovered is that both groups valued the forest and wanted to preserve it for future generations. That became their shared goal. The challenge existed at the subgroup level because each group viewed the other with hostility and suspicion. They eventually came to an agreement, but one that maintained the values of both groups. They did this by adopting a new social identity that shifted away from their divergent affiliations to a more collective and inclusive affiliation within their local community. So, for example, the loggers began to see the environmentalists as part of their community. As their definition of the community expanded, this changed the context of the conflict and allowed for more effective negotiation of their differences. Something similar will be needed in order to address deeply felt differences within the body of Christ.

Earlier, we suggested that Paul engaged in a process of re-categorization, and he did so without negating subgroup identities. Rather, he recognized the legitimacy of subgroup identities so that the formation of a more inclusive social identity could occur. While it seems strange that Paul legitimated the slave's identity, he did so with qualifications (see also 1 Cor. 7:20–22). He asks Philemon to view Onesimus "no longer as a slave" (Philem. 16). If Paul wanted to say this subgroup identity (or social status) was abrogated, he probably would not have included "as."[14] Its presence in this phrase indicates Paul's subjective perspective of Onesimus's identity. He is a slave, yet he has been transformed into "more than a slave" (v. 16 NRSV). His existing status has been recategorized to a more inclusive level of saliency as "a beloved brother." Thus, Paul identifies him in the context of his existing identity as a "slave" and his transformed identity in Christ as "a beloved brother."

One might argue that Onesimus would have preferred to be identified only as "a beloved brother" so his slave identity could be abrogated. Yet the social dynamics involved did not make this a valid option. Paul's primary purpose was reconciliation, and we'll see below the way he effects this. However, Philemon had the upper hand in this relationship, and Paul was quite concerned to address the deformations of his identity.

Paul as an Entrepreneur of Philemon's Dual Identities

While the recategorization of Onesimus is important, the negotiation of Philemon's social identities appears to be another concern for Paul. Philemon had sent Onesimus to Paul as a gift likely designed to entangle Paul in a further patronage relationship, the dominant socioeconomic model in antiquity, given the prevalence of patronage language in the letter (vv. 1, 7, 13, 17, and 22). For example, Paul notes that Philemon's house is used for community gatherings that would have entailed several behaviors associated with patronage (v. 2). It seems the primary problem here was Philemon seeking to maintain an existing economic structure that was somewhat incompatible with the social implications of the gospel. His economic identity needed to be transformed.

However, Paul, in another sense, acts like a patron in relation to Philemon. This may also suggest that Paul builds on an existing economic structure but seeks to transform it within the Christ movement. First, he reminds Philemon that it was based on Paul's ministry that he was originally converted, and thus he clearly owes Paul something (v. 19b). Second, Paul describes the way Philemon is obligated to "serve" him (v. 13 ESV). Third, Paul and Philemon relate to one another according to hierarchy (vv. 8–9, 13, 19b, 21, 22). Thus, both Philemon and Onesimus were part of a "nested social dilemma," one that could potentially hinder Paul's mission if it was not resolved adequately.[15] Philemon and Onesimus needed to be recategorized, not obliterating but transforming subgroup identities so that their shared superordinate identity as brothers increased in salience, resulting in positive interdependence and securing the continuance of the Pauline mission among them.

Paul still views Onesimus as a slave since that was his legal situation. Paul does, however, see a transformation in Onesimus's identity. He is a slave *and* a beloved brother in Christ. And the former does not prevent him from being the latter. In v. 16b, Paul provides an evaluation of Onesimus and connects him to himself and to a greater degree to Philemon ("how much more to you"). Haslam contends that the "dual identity model," which is based on the premise of social identity salience, "need not suppress individuality or sub-group specialization—it can simply harness these things towards a common goal."[16] Onesimus was earlier described as one who was "useless" but had been transformed into one who was now "useful" to both Paul and Philemon (v. 11).

What we find in this profound letter is that existing social identities continue to maintain their fundamental significance within the Christ movement. Paul's phrase in v. 16, "both in the flesh and in the Lord" (ESV), seems to support this. Paul uses this phrase to recategorize Onesimus's identity in relation to

Philemon. Philemon relates to Onesimus as his owner ("in the flesh") and as a brother ("in the Lord"). In other words, these phrases are not describing discrete domains but are inclusive descriptors of life within the Christ movement as Paul sees it.[17]

So, did Paul want Philemon to free Onesimus? In light of Paul's teaching in 1 Corinthians 7:17–24, he did. For Paul, existing identities continue to be relevant within the body of Christ. However, there are exceptions to this rule, as evinced in 1 Corinthians 7:20–22. In Philemon 17 and 21, Paul asks for Onesimus to be freed so he can serve Paul in his mission. Paul was *not* seeking to reinscribe Roman socioeconomic dominance via its slave economy, and any use of his arguments throughout history to support slavery or racism were and are wrongheaded. Such arguments misunderstand not only Paul's anthropology, since all humans are made equally in the image of God (Gen. 1:27), but also his teaching that one's identity is transformed in Christ and is thus a member of Christ's body (1 Cor. 3:23).

In this situation, Paul was helping Philemon understand the way aspects of his social identity were to be transformed within the body of Christ. He also wanted Philemon to understand how one's identity transformation in Christ impacts the way he viewed and evaluated others. Onesimus's identity as a slave remains, but it is not his superordinate or master identity. Paul was helping Philemon understand not only Onesimus's dual identities but also how Philemon now relates to Onesimus in a twofold way: "in the flesh and in the Lord" (v. 16 ESV). The fact that Onesimus is a "brother" impacts the way Philemon should relate to him. Thus, in Paul's letter, we find four points of action that help us today in seeking to reduce conflict: "working towards a larger goal, creating equal status, engaging in personal interaction, and providing leadership."[18]

Returning to 1 Corinthians, we find Paul's imagery of the body of Christ described the way individual and social identities interrelate in the church. It also addressed the divisions created by allowing their congregational life to be influenced by cultural assumptions about status. Once the Corinthians realized that they all ultimately belong to Christ and share an equal status in Him, then they could see social differences as opportunities for mission. In the body of Christ, the status of the poor can be reversed as the rich change their approach to table fellowship, and the plight of slaves can be transformed as slave owners recognize the social implications of gospel. Paul's understanding of union with Christ brings together the theological and the social. Thomas Howard describes this transformed approach to life this way: "The Incarnation took all that properly belongs to our humanity and delivered it back to us, redeemed. All of our inclinations and appetites and capacities and yearnings and proclivities are purified and gathered up and glorified by Christ. He did not come to thin out human life; He came to set it free."[19] Paul knew that the Corinthians and Philemon needed a transformed vision of life in the body of Christ, since that was crucial for human flourishing and unity within the church. While those in Christ still retain their distinct individual identities, they all are one in Christ.

So, what's the way forward today in helping our churches realize and maintain our oneness in Christ? First, leaders should help their congregations see that group affiliations are not bad per se. They are a natural part of what it means to be human. Second, look for ways to teach how the New Testament focuses on group-based issues and their importance for effective ministry. Third, do the hard work of uncovering the way existing cultural affiliations are dividing your local body, and in an irenic fashion, share those findings. Fourth, emphasize through your preaching and teaching of the Word that the most important identity a person has is their membership in the body of Christ. Their personal identity, while important, must be subservient to who they are in Christ. Fifth, seek creative ways to develop openness to difference and cultural flexibility in the church. Finally, work with the three key tools of social identity leadership: (1) cast a compelling vision of identity for the group through your use of language; (2) remind your people of this identity in the various meetings, celebrations, memorials, and rituals involved in congregational life; (3) engineer new structures and mobilize the church to social action. This also involves the formation of new leaders who will embody this shared vision for a congregation that is unified in the context of their individual identities. These tools suggest that ministry leaders need to think more concretely about their role as managers of the identity of the congregation. It is to this we now turn.

Questions for Reflection

1. How does Paul's imagery of the body of Christ help us understand the goal of maintaining unity amid diversity?

2. Being open to difference and culturally flexible are two crucial tools for maintaining unity in the church. What kinds of people do you think your church finds difficult to accept? Why is this the case? What steps might your church take to change this?

3. Can you think of ways that churches or Christians "fossilize" their identity? How can this be overcome?

4. Paul, Philemon, and Onesimus were mixed up in a sticky social relationship. Can you think of a similar situation that might occur today? If so, how might seeing each other "in the flesh and in the Lord" (ESV) help the individuals resolve their conflict?

6

RACE, ETHNICITY, AND IDENTITY

Existing social, racial, and ethnic identities are areas of church disunity. The Bible's vision of being all together within a context of God-given differences is often unfulfilled because of our strong preference to be with those who are like us—and even because of prejudices. In North America, evangelical congregations continue to be self-segregated. These monocultural experiences often contribute to misunderstandings in contemporary political policies and actions. Ethnic differences between various subgroups create further segmentation, and sin enters this segmentation to create alienation and misunderstanding, and thus deforming identities. As Al Mohler explains, "The separation of humans into ranks of superiority and inferiority differentiated by skin color is a direct assault on the doctrine of creation and an insult to the *imago Dei*, the image of God in which every human is made. Racial superiority is also directly subversive of the gospel of Christ, effectively denying the full power of his substitutionary atonement and undermining the faithful preaching of the gospel to all persons and . . . all nations."[1] Concerning racial and ethnic discrimination in United States history, we have much to grieve over and repent of. Progress has been made, yet much remains to be done. For this, an understanding of our social identity in Christ becomes crucial.

One of the problems posed for us in formulating a biblical response to remaining racial and ethnic discrimination is the contextual differences between the biblical setting and the contemporary world. We are also hindered by a universalistic approach to Christian identity that argues existing social identities are irrelevant in the church—such as "your old life, your old identity is dead."[2] What we need is a nuanced understanding of the relationship between Christian identity and ethnicity.

Pastor Tony Evans offers a way forward: "The church is the place where racial, gender, and class distinctions are no longer to be divisive because of our unity in Christ (Galatians 3:28). This does not negate differences that remain intact—oneness simply means that those differences are embraced."[3]

This approach could be described as the particularistic approach to Christian identity. It sees a continuation of particular existing social, racial, and ethnic identities in Christ. Racial and ethnic identities are types of social identities and are central to a person's self-understanding. In a North American context, racial identity is often based on biological differences such as skin color or other physical features. While ethnic identity might include these, it tends to highlight the cultural components of embodiment. There is always some level of transformation that occurs regarding these identities because of the continued presence of sin, but to claim that one's life before Christ has been obliterated and thus rendered passé, or that we should ignore racial and ethnic differences because we're all in Christ, is problematic. Timothy Keller's observation is also helpful:

> The Christian who makes Christ and his love the core of his or her identity, then, discovers that we need not completely reject other identity factors. Our race and national identity, our work and profession, our family and politics and community ties can all remain intact. They are no longer the ultimate basis for our significance and security, but that does not mean they are flattened or eliminated. Rather we are free to enjoy them as God's gifts to us, but we are no longer enslaved to them as our saviors.[4]

Let's look at some of the key findings from social identity research and Paul's writings so we can discover a way of understanding Christian identity that embraces differences as good gifts of God. As a result, we will understand better how to pursue and maintain Christian unity while honoring individual differences.

IDENTITY HIERARCHY, SALIENCE, AND CULTURE CREATION

Thus far, it should be clear that every person has multiple identities existing in a hierarchy and that he or she is able to prioritize key aspects of who they are depending on the situation. The priority can shift based on changing situations, and when this occurs, the resulting reorganization establishes which identity will be acted out. An example of a hypothetical identity hierarchy for a person like Stephanas in first-century Corinth would be: a husband, a father, a client to Gaius, a patron to Crispus, an urban shopkeeper, a slave owner, and a member of the body of Christ. It's easy to see how some of these aspects of his identity could conflict with one another.

One key element of an identity hierarchy is the presence of a master identity. For Paul, one's identity as a member of the body of Christ must be the master identity, which informs all other identities. Some Christians in Corinth continued to identify primarily with their Roman social identity instead of their identity in Christ. This caused disunity within the Christ community there. Paul urged them to reorganize their identity hierarchy to produce an alternative community with a distinct ethos. This is the kind of cultural change we alluded to in the introduction, which is direly needed in churches today.

THE CONTINUATION OF ETHNIC IDENTITIES IN 1 CORINTHIANS

Interpreters of 1 Corinthians often see existing identities as something that has been obliterated in Christ.[5] Ethnic differences are thought to be the source of divisions. The actual problem, however, is sin. As a member of a first-century minority ethnic group, Paul understood the negative impact ethnic indifference could produce. Israel's identity was constantly under the threat of assimilation, which would have disastrous results for their calling as a "light to the nations" (Isa. 49:6 NRSV). So, Paul sought to partially fulfill this vocation in his mission to the nations, a mission that maintained the continued salience of ethnic identities (Acts 13:46–47; Rom. 1:16). This may be described as a mission of social identification. Paul was well aware that existing identities played into the formation of congregations, and he capitalized on those dynamics while resisting the influence of Roman social identities that were incongruous with the gospel (see 1 Cor. 2:6–9; 7:31; 2 Cor. 4:4; Phil. 3:20; 1 Thess. 5:3). As mentioned in the introduction, ignoring the influence of the dominant culture only reinforces its power because in doing so, we fail to understand what is merely cultural and what is integral to Christian identity.

Those who study the emergence of Christianity in Africa have sought to understand and disentangle what is central to Christian identity and what is only a vestige of European cultural identity. Categorization, as we saw earlier, is essential to the way humans relate to the world. Thus, the goal isn't to eliminate this cognitive process but to ensure it occurs through the work of the Spirit and the formation of the mind of Christ (1 Cor. 2:14–16; Rom. 12:1–2). Paul even recognizes this in 1 Corinthians 11:19: "No doubt there have to be differences among you to show which of you have God's approval." The goal in the creation of a transformed culture is not the elimination of differences but the submission of all aspects of our identity under the lordship of Christ. Ultimately, we belong to Him (1 Cor. 3:23). One's ethnic, cultural, or social identities are key indicators for social categorization and serve as indispensable aspects of the "fellowship" to which we've been called (1 Cor. 1:9). Four examples will show how Paul affirmed the continuation of these identities in 1 Corinthians.

First, ethnic distinctions are crucial to Paul's overall argument in 1 Corinthians. In 1 Corinthians 1:22–24, Paul writes,

"Jews demand signs and Greeks look for wisdom, but we preach Christ crucified: a stumbling block to Jews and foolishness to Gentiles, but to those whom God has called, both Jews and Greeks, Christ the power of God and the wisdom of God." These verses should be seen as Paul's instructions regarding behaviors associated with ethnic groups that are functioning too high in the identity hierarchy. Paul indicates that these characteristics need to be reevaluated in Christ, who has become the power and wisdom of God. Paul is not disparaging Greek pursuits of wisdom or Jewish longing for power. He is recategorizing both within a context of being called by God (1 Cor. 1:24). Prioritizing God's call helps us to process information about ourselves and others.

Second, ethnic distinctions continue for Paul as a matter of calling. In 1 Cor. 7:18–20, Paul continues, "Was a man already circumcised when he was called? He should not become uncircumcised. Was a man uncircumcised when he was called? He should not be circumcised. Circumcision is nothing and uncircumcision is nothing. Keeping God's commands is what counts. Each person should remain in the situation they were in when God called them." In these verses, calling continues to serve as that which enables us to reorient our cultural context and social life. Ethnic identity markers such as circumcision and uncircumcision are not eliminated but are reprioritized. This reordering occurs as Paul teaches the community to stay in the social situation they were in when they began to follow Christ. He does not call the community to discontinue practices associated with their ethnic identity but simply reminds them that "keeping God's commands" is what's most important (1 Cor. 7:19; Gal. 5:6; 6:15). This suggests that some transformation might be in order regarding one's ethnic identity, especially if one boasts in their cultural identity.

Third, ethnic differences continue to be relevant in Christ. In 1 Corinthians 10:32, Paul argues that ethnic differentiation is still relevant for those who are in Christ. Communal behavior choices should be made with social identity in view: "Do not cause anyone to stumble, whether Jews, Greeks or the church of God." He encourages the community not to offend Jews or Greeks—that is, those who are not in Christ and who associate exclusively with those of their own ethnic identity. Paul also tells them not to offend those within God's community. This verse, therefore, could be understood as referring to both those outside the Christ movement (Jews and Greeks) *and* those inside it. Or, more likely, one could understand the term typically translated "or" or "and" to mean "even." This verse could thus be rendered: "Jews and Greeks, even those belonging to the church." Ethnicity is still a valid marker of identity even for those following Christ. Therefore, as Christians, we need to pay attention to the way we talk and live in light of various ethnic groups in our cultural context.

Fourth, the recognition of existing ethnic identities is crucial for the unity of Christ's body. In 1 Corinthians 12:13, Paul argues for the unity of the body in the context of ethnic definition: "For we were all baptized by one Spirit so as to form one body—whether Jews or Gentiles, slave or free—and we were all given the one Spirit to drink." This verse does not mean that social categories disappear once we are in Christ. Instead, they are realigned within the context of our baptismal identity. As mentioned earlier, Paul's goal in writing was to persuade those in Christ to adjust their current social identity hierarchy. This transformation results in an identity that is rooted in the understanding that the community belongs to Christ. That is the kind of congregational culture Paul was seeking to form. But what does it mean to have a salient social identity of being in Christ?

SALIENT IN-CHRIST IDENTITIES

The Greater Bellevue Baptist Church in Macon, Georgia became an internet sensation because of a fight during a service. The fight was captured on a video showing attendees throwing chairs at each other, body-slamming one another, throwing haymaker punches, and utterly destroying the sanctuary space in which they had gathered to worship. Some people were even arrested. The conflict began when accusations of sinful behavior were leveled against the leadership.

We might take a kind of misguided comfort from such an extreme example of disunity and thank God we are not like those hostile congregants. But all churches struggle with conflict in some form or another. Some who seem to be at peace may merely keep it underground, expressing their anger toward one another in passive-aggressive behavior. This is not just a contemporary problem, of course. Paul had to address something similar in 1 Corinthians 6:1 when church members were taking each other to court. Part of the problem was the way the Corinthian believers misunderstood the nature of their past and current life in Christ and the way they should relate to one another in a community comprised of differing social classes (see 1 Cor. 6:7, 11). This continues to be a problem for the church today. What we need is a transformed understanding of what it means to be in Christ, so we can not only avoid the public embarrassment of YouTube church fights but truly live as Christ has called us to live. That's the focus of identity salience—living as Christ has called us to live.

As mentioned earlier in chapter 3, being in Christ has both objective and subjective components. It refers to our union with Christ objectively: "whoever is united with the Lord is one with him in spirit" (1 Cor. 6:17). It is a summary concept that incorporates the various aspects of our salvation. The subjective aspects are variously described, but the idea of sanctification is often brought to the fore in Paul's letters (Rom. 6:11–13; Phil. 2:12–13). Those in Christ progressively experience the benefits of their union with Christ in an ongoing and transformative way (2 Cor. 3:18). This is a biblical way to describe the needed transformation of some existing identities. Civic identity was a problem for the Corinthians, and something similar can cause problems for us today. The reason we need to think about this issue more holistically is that we otherwise don't allow God's Word to penetrate the way our cultural upbringing adversely affects us.

One Sunday morning, on the weekend for the commemoration of Dr. Martin Luther King Jr. Day, the choir I (Brian) once led sang an arrangement of "Free At Last" that included a video clip of part of King's "I Have a Dream" speech. After the service, a church member came up to me, clearly frustrated with something. I asked him if he was okay, and his response shocked me: "Based on this morning's choir song, I guess you'll sing a song honoring 'Groundhog Day' next?" This individual clearly had not allowed the renovating work of the Holy Spirit to change his racist attitudes and actions. As leaders, we need to think theologically about existing identities, which then allows us to address issues that otherwise might be left unaddressed.

Paul's approach to community formation provides wisdom for leaders in the midst of the messiness of cultural moments and misunderstandings based on racial and ethnic experiences. One African American student of mine was reminded of something his mother used to tell him about the role of the church in the formation of African American identity during the mid-twentieth-century South:

> "In the world," black folks were demeaned and denigrated. Our level of education and training wasn't recognized in the job market. We went to separate schools that used hand-me-down materials from the white schools. We used separate water fountains, went in separate entrances to restaurants and department stores. We were so peppered with indignity, that the church was the one place that we could find dignity. Not only the highest dignity from God, but also in the fellowship with brothers and sisters in Christ. So we really dressed up for church. And we would stay there all day; partly for worship services, partly for social events. We were given titles that dignified us: Reverend, Pastor, Deacon, Mother . . . even just Brother or Sister. The church was the hub of Southern, African American identity.

The traditional approach to church unity is not equipped to handle the importance of this type of contextualization. It is also quite likely that the apostle Paul would essentially say, "The gospel is flexible enough to fill in these diverse cultural contexts with God's glory" (see 1 Cor. 10:31). This means that our corporate worship should help bring our cultural, racial, and ethnic identities into focus. One implication of this is that we may need to change some of the worship songs we sing. Too often, songs highlight our future in heaven or include lines like "Turn your eyes upon Jesus, look full at his wonderful face, and the things of earth will grow strangely dim." I would suggest that while the sentiments of this song in relation to Jesus' supremacy are crucial, if your worship causes the details of this world to grow dim, your thinking and song selection need to be transformed. Otherwise you may lose your passion for evangelism, downplay your responsibility in light of the cultural mandate, or cloister yourself in holy huddles, seeking to escape the harsh realities of contemporary life. One way to do this is to balance these with songs like "This Is My Father's World," in which we sing, "This is my Father's world, and to my listening ears, all nature sings, and round me rings, the music of the spheres." Our worship should bring the world in which we live into focus. My goal isn't to ruin your favorite worship songs but to help you recognize the importance of worship lyrics and what they say about our approach to cultural engagement.

Building a unified gospel-based church culture is a messy endeavor. Neat, cookie-cutter approaches are unlikely to generate flourishing congregations. This is not a new problem. Paul faced something quite similar in his ministry to the Ephesian church. His solution was not to obliterate existing identities but to remind the Jewish and non-Jewish believers there that they all shared a common identity in Christ.

THE CONTINUATION
OF ETHNIC IDENTITIES IN EPHESIANS

Ephesians 2:11–22 provides an early example of the way Paul communicated the social implications of the gospel across cultural contexts and what that means for discipleship. However, not all interpreters see this passage this way. Some believe Paul suggests that existing ethnic identities are removed in the "one new man" (Eph. 2:14 ESV), while others think that gentiles are called to identify themselves in Christ alone to the complete exclusion of their host culture.[6] Evans's summary of this passage is helpful: "God has reconciled racially divided groups into one new man (Eph. 2:14–15), uniting them into a new body (Eph. 2:16) so that the church can function in unity (Eph. 4:13)."[7] While it's not in our purview to offer a complete analysis of this passage, we will draw several principles from it to show that identifying with God's people doesn't erase existing ethnic identities. Put another way, being in Christ does not lead to a "raceless race."[8] Racial and ethnic reconciliation should be sought within the context of these identities instead of to the exclusion of them.

This is challenging because these identities function differently based on the situation and the comparison group. Martin Scorsese highlights this challenge in the documentary *New York*. His parents grew up in the tenements in New York and lived across the street from one another. One was from a town in Sicily near Palermo, and the other was from a different Italian town also outside of Palermo but higher in the mountains. When Scorsese's mother met his father, their families considered each other to be of a different nationality. Those who are not members of these groups likely miss these nuances and can inadvertently offend people by making thoughtless comments.

Living in community with those who relate to Christ in the context of their existing identities often requires more work from those who are members of the majority group. This means following Christ with open-minded humility and a willingness to change our thoughts and language about others. One of my colleagues alerted me that the way I was using the labels "Asian" and "Hispanic" overlooked crucial subgroup distinctions of which I was unaware. And another colleague reminded me that when we are taking about racism, what we are usually talking about is the way minority groups in the United States are trying to figure out how to get along with white people. I know that may be hard to hear, but these God-given differences are part of His good creation and should lead to human flourishing, not conflict. The Ephesians wrestled with this, too.

Paul reminds the Ephesians of an important social implication of the gospel: "For he himself is our peace, who has made the two groups one and has destroyed the barrier, the dividing wall of hostility, by setting aside in his flesh the law with its commands and regulations. His purpose was to create in himself one new humanity out of the two, thus making peace" (2:14–15). Sin, as the deformer of identity, has produced hostility between people groups (Gen. 3:15), and God's instructions for Israel's unique and holy identity among the nations often resulted in separation and hostility between Jews and gentile— though it's likely that the "commands and regulations" here refer to later additions like the inscription warning non-Jews not to enter the Temple Mount, a prohibition not evident in Israel's Scriptures. Regardless, the key question is whether the "one new humanity" obliterates existing identities like Jew and gentile. Paul says Jews and gentiles in Christ form one body—they are co-citizens of the "commonwealth of Israel" (Eph. 2:12, 19 ESV).[9] However, gentiles themselves do not become Israelites (2:12, 19; 3:6). This is similar to the way members of the British Commonwealth maintained their unique identity from their country of birth (Canada, for example) along with a superordinate British one. In the same way, gentiles in Christ are heirs together with Israel, "members of the same body, and partakers of the promise in Christ Jesus" (3:6).

Ephesians 2:15b in the NRSV reads, "that he might create in himself one new humanity in place of the two, thus making peace." The NRSV unfortunately gives the impression that a replacement has occurred. The Greek, however, does not indicate "in place of." In order for the Greek to be translated coherently into English, something needed to be added in order to connect "the two" with the "one new humanity." The NIV rendering, "out of the two," is better because it suggests that the respective identities of the two groups remain intact. Bible scholar Markus Barth contends that the "one new man . . . consists of two, that is, Jews and Gentiles . . . Jews are yet not paganized, and the Gentiles not 'forced to judaize' (Gal 2:14) in order to be 'one in Christ.' Their historic distinction remains true and recognized even within their communion."[10] Based on this reading, ethnic identities continue within the "one new humanity." This is reinforced in the second part of Ephesians, where various instructions are given with continuing social identities in view (5:22–33). Similar "one flesh" language is used in 5:31, where Paul concretizes his teaching in 2:15 concerning the way differing ethnic identities continue to be relevant though reprioritized in Christ.

The Roman household code in 4:21–6:9 is one of the clearest examples of the way existing identities continue in a reprioritized manner within the Christ movement. Paul builds on the continuation of existing Roman social identities in forming the community. This could have been a wise communication strategy—drawing from familiar ideas—or, more likely, it may represent a way in which first-century Christ followers were explicitly not required to leave their Roman culture behind. Instead, they were to define their ongoing in-Christ experience within the context of their Roman culture, rather than to the exclusion of it.

At the same time, we may need to put aside some aspects of our ongoing social identities. Paul never encourages a wholesale embrace of Roman social identity. Ephesians 2:11 and 4:17 provide ample evidence for the discontinuation of significant aspects of gentile identity for those who are in Christ. The claim here is not that gentile identity continues unabated in Christ. Certain social identities may continue unless there are other mitigating circumstances—such as immorality, idolatry, unscriptural thought patterns, and cultural boasting. The mixture of unscriptural thought patterns and cultural boasting were highlighted for me in a story that one of my former students shared with me. He wrote,

> I work in a predominately African-American neighborhood in Detroit with a church that is mostly white. The past year has been quite difficult with the election of President Trump. Political tensions have been exacerbated with Facebook. It was once the case, whether good or bad, that people came to church and left political talk outside the door. But it is only natural for church members to

become friends on Facebook, and then thoughts are shared more easily. But some sharing can be done without thinking of who is reading it. One member, for example, posted a meme saying "Obamacare only works for those who don't." I approached this individual and explained that our family benefits from Obamacare (and actually, at the time, we had just phased out of Medicare!). He responded, "Well, that wasn't said with you in mind." But when we discussed other members of the church, whom he knew, and whom I knew to benefit from Obamacare, then he stated he didn't have those people in mind either! This eventually led to a public apology on his part (via Facebook). It's one thing to have a generic "other" in mind, but when faces are associated with "these people," that's a different story. This is a time when I felt that genuinely opening up about hurtful words, combined with actual fellowship with people who are different, led to a positive change. While no one's mind was changed on politics (honoring our unique identities), the experience did lead to a greater appreciation of the complexities involved in living together in fellowship.

My former student helped his fellow church attendee see that the influence of cultural boasting and unscriptural thought patterns were contributing to a lack of following Christ holistically. The social implications of the gospel cover all areas of life.

In Ephesians 2:11, the addressees are reminded that they used to be "Gentiles in the flesh." The use of "flesh" here is neutral, not negative as it is in 2:3 (ESV). (The NIV gives this sense when it translates the phrase "Gentiles by birth.") The phrase is employed as an identity marker for a male non-Israelite, similar to "uncircumcision." The term *circumcision* is used for an Israelite male later in the verse. With the physical markers of identity still intact, these Ephesian believers continued to be "Gentiles in the flesh," but were now also transformed by Christ into "fellow heirs, members of the same body, and partakers of the promise in Christ through the gospel" (3:6 ESV). In 4:17, the addressees are instructed to "no longer live as the Gentiles live." On the surface, this could sound as if existing ethnic and social identities no longer have a place within the Christ movement. However, "Gentiles" here refers to those aspects of their previous life that were incompatible with their new identity in Christ and thus required change. It does not follow that Paul no longer considered them to be gentiles in Christ. What is occurring in 2:11 and 4:17 is a kind of reinvention of the gentile label as a micro-identity describing their pre-Christian lifestyle and pointing to the transformation that should evidence itself within the church. For Paul, gentiles in Christ continue to be gentiles, and Jews in Christ continue to be Jews. Paul isn't destroying ethnic and social identities but rather sees them as part of God's good creation.

In *Rescuing the Gospel from the Cowboys*, the late Native American author Richard Twiss wrestled with the destruction of worlds that occurred in the North American setting as the gospel was taken to Native Americans. He shared how he had to wrestle with the way his Native American identity related to his in-Christ identity. The advice he was given was that in light of Galatians 3:28, he shouldn't worry about his Native identity. Instead, he was told to "just become like us." The problem was the "becoming like us" was a cultural mismatch that resulted from conflating the gospel with North American culture.

Now, all cultures need transformation, so we are not arguing for full-blown acceptance of the status quo. Rather, we want to highlight the struggle that Native Americans wrestle with as they discern what it means to follow Christ and retain their socio-ethnic identity.[11]

The differences between those in the church are most evident when it comes to race and ethnicity. Ethnic differences were one reason for the church's first internal conflict. The complaint of those who had adopted gentile culture against those who retained the culture associated with their Jewish heritage was rooted in a long-standing ethnic divide (Acts 15:1–6). Ethnic differences are larger than race and may reflect cultural practices as well as physical characteristics. However, racial identity often highlights our differences in a way that makes it difficult for some to include others or be included. This difficulty becomes a special problem when these differences are viewed as a mark of inferiority, both by those who do not possess them and by those who do. While the early church did not ignore ethnic and racial differences, its response combined theological construction with practical understanding.

So, how can maintaining the salience of existing ethnic and racial identities help in upholding the unity of the church? It provides a new way of thinking about the way to resolve conflict that is often based on these identities. When a church finds itself in conflict, it is because people have aligned themselves in groups against one another. One traditional way to resolve this is for leaders to downplay distinct social categories that are present and focus only on individual issues. This is referred to as decategorization, and it will not resolve large-scale problems. Another approach is recategorization, in which the group distinctions are recognized but downplayed, and everyone is treated as part of a common group. This is a better approach than the first. But all too often, the minority group's identity is not actually valued, and the so-called resolutions tend to reinforce the status quo. The most effective model is the dual-identity one, in which distinct identities are recognized and accommodated with the larger group identity. This allows for the ongoing recognition of the actual problems at the lower level while seeking resolution and reconciliation at the level of what is shared—in this case, their membership in the body of Christ. Obviously this is harder than decategorization and recategorization, since it requires looking for new possibilities for old problems, making concessions that are often uncomfortable, and bridging between groups so that the outcome aligns with the priorities of each group. To do this, leaders need to spend a significant amount of time listening and understanding what the actual identity-based issues are, rather than setting them aside as irrelevant to congregational life. The move from the initial point of contention to an integrative solution travels along the line of negotiating subgroup and master identities.[12]

The approach to church conflict resolution suggested here recognizes the role existing identities have in church conflicts and seeks to bring those under the lordship of Christ by providing a theological vision of the conflict and defining the boundaries, support, and communal framework for life together. Pastors and church leaders are wise to keep four ideas in mind: (1) maintain an awareness of all the existing identities involved; (2) provide a theological vision for the conflict; (3) define biblically the group's superordinate identity and goal; and (4) establish boundaries, interdependence, and the centrality of an in-Christ identity.

The following points of action will prove additionally fruitful:

1. Humbly consider our own potential for perpetuating negative attitudes about other groups.
2. Recognize that some negative stereotypes about a subgroup may be accurate and based on social injustices that need to be addressed.
3. Realize that even if a negative stereotype is accurate, it doesn't necessary apply in an absolute way to all members of a subgroup.
4. Consider the centrality of reconciliation (Luke 10:27).
5. Remember we are called to a ministry of reconciliation (2 Cor. 5:18).
6. Increase efforts to be in relationships of interdependence with subgroups other than your own.
7. Recognize that contact by itself does not reduce prejudice.
8. Be mindful of media messages we've been exposed to with regard to other groups.
9. Consider the negative messages we've received from our relatives and friends.
10. Realize that reconciliation efforts are most productive when pursued collectively.
11. Remember that forgiveness, repentance, and reconciliation are integral to God's redeeming work in the world.
12. Work to accept our common humanity and our unique cultural identities, as noted by Tony Evans.

Combined, these offer practical ways to navigate
the contact zone of racial and ethnic identities.[13]

In the midst of racial and ethnic divisions, it's easy to lose hope that anything can change, but church leaders should be encouraged because the power of the gospel is sufficient to overcome even the most entrenched ethnic-based conflicts (Eph. 2:14). This means there's a role for ministry leaders in forging the character of our society through the work of the local church. This calls for an expanded understanding of God's kingdom as we engage, listen to, and empathize with those who have suffered injustices. The gospel has social, political, cultural, personal, and religious ramifications that need to be uncovered. This expansive view may allow us to participate with the Holy Spirit in fighting evils such as racism and xeno-phobia through a praxis-based proclamation of the gospel of Christ and the coming kingdom of God.

Questions for Reflection

1. Why do you think churches continue to be so segregated based on racial and ethnic identities?
2. What benefits might a congregation receive from greater racial and ethnic diversity? What challenges would it face?
3. What is a "master" identity?
4. How would you be able to tell whether your in-Christ identity is functioning as your master

identity? What practical steps might you take to make this a reality?

5. What role should Christians and the church play in racial and ethnic reconciliation in our society? How might we use Paul's guidance in Ephesians 2 in a ministry of reconciliation?

NEITHER MALE NOR FEMALE

If you went through the public school system, you probably remember "the talk." It took place around seventh grade, and the fact that boys and girls were separated and taken to different locations was the first clue that something unusual was going on. Some of us had a heads up about what was going to happen from the whispers and giggles of older friends or siblings. But for most of us, it came as an awkward surprise. The topic was the miracle of life. Actually, "miracle" is probably not the best word to use. God wasn't a part of the presentation. The talk was really all about biology. We watched a film about how babies come into the world, and then a teacher entertained uncomfortable and sometimes cynical questions from the young audience. Schools still hold "the talk." But most come to the assembly today with far more information than their parents and grandparents did.

Sex has always been a feature of culture. But today, we are immersed in it. It is hard to find a context in popular culture where sex is not at least a subtext of the conversation. From the movies and television shows we watch to the music we hear and advertising we see, sex is used to capture our attention. Hardcore pornography is only a few clicks away on the home computer—or smartphone—and the kinds of images considered normal on the web today would have been deemed more appropriate for *Playboy* a few decades ago.

We are naïve to think we aren't being affected by any of this. In their book, *So Sexy So Soon*, Diane Levin and Jean Kilbourne describe how one mother found her seven-year-old daughter, Hannah, crying in the bathtub. "I'm fat! I'm fat!" Hannah wept. "I want to be pretty like Isabelle—sexy like her! Then Judd would like me too."[1] In an article, Kilbourne explains that this isn't just a "girl" thing. Advertising regularly treats both sexes like "things." "Women's bodies—and men's bodies, too, these days—are dismembered, packaged and used to sell everything from chainsaws to chewing gum, champagne to shampoo," she explains. These images do more than capture attention, they shape our identity—but in a most destructive way. "The self-esteem of girls plummets as they reach adolescence partly because they cannot possibly escape the message that their bodies are objects, and imperfect objects at that. Boys learn that masculinity requires a kind of ruthlessness, even brutality."[2]

The power of these messages comes from the fact that they are conveyed to us "off the radar" through advertising. We are passive and receptive when exposed to them because we think that since it's only advertising we are immune to its effects. We know a sales pitch when we see one. Or do we?

Kilbourne warns that the effectiveness of advertising lies in the fact that its impact is cumulative, subtle, and unconscious:

"A former editor-in-chief of *Advertising Age*, the leading advertising publication in North America, once claimed: 'Only eight per cent of an ad's message is received by the conscious mind. The rest is worked and re-worked deep within, in the recesses of the brain.'"[3]

Popular media and advertising both shape and reflect our culture's changing values. The clear message of today's media is that the nature of sexuality itself has changed. Sex is not only about being sexy or having sex. On a more basic level, it is about what it means to be male or female. These are questions about cultural norms. But more fundamentally, they are questions of human identity. The LGBTQ movement has changed the way many in today's culture think about what it means to be male and female. In the process, they have redefined sex as gender, transforming it from something fixed into a social construct and a personal choice. This cultural shift makes it difficult to discern what's malleable and what's defined by God when it comes to our notions of male and female.

In the past, sex was defined as the physiological distinction between male and female. Gender was commonly defined culturally as the set of rules or norms that apply to each. One's sex was fixed. The rules of gender were not. Both factors play an important role in shaping sexual identity. Today's culture has detached sex from physiology. Many believe that whether one considers themselves to be male or female is merely a matter of personal perception and choice. Some are even suggesting that it's unfair to assign a sex to a child until they are old enough to decide which sex they want to be. However, the Bible affirms the fixed nature of sexual identity and links it with physiology.

CREATED MALE AND FEMALE

One of the first truths we learn about human identity in Scripture is that it has a sexual dimension. The first thing we're told about humanity's creation in the image of God in Genesis 1:27 is that God created humans "male and female." Down through the centuries, theologians have pondered the significance of the detail. What does God's image have to do with humanity's sexual nature? Male and female reflect the image but are probably not the image itself. "Even if the image were indeed defined by the phrase *male and female*, it would still be unclear what exactly this means for a doctrine of the *imago Dei*," Bible scholar Richard Middleton observes. Middleton believes the phrase "male and female" anticipates the commission given to them in v. 28.[4]

In other words, being male or female is not itself the image of God but is central to what it means for us to fulfill our vocation as those who reflect God's image. This much is clear in the Genesis account: God created humanity to be binary in its sexual identity. But the implications of this sexual differentiation are more than functional. There is a social design implied as well.

When Paul speaks of the relationship between male and female in 1 Corinthians 11, he notes that God designed the two sexes to be interdependent: "Nevertheless, in the Lord woman is not independent of man, nor is man independent of woman. For as woman came from man, so also man is born of woman. But everything comes from God" (1 Cor. 11:11–12). This statement qualifies the directives given in the previous verses about gender and authority in the church. While there is a gendered order that places authority in the hands of males, neither male nor female can afford to view the other with contempt.

Theologian Karl Barth sees this mutual dependence as the key to understanding sexual identity. "The serious purpose of what makes the male, male is that according to the saying of the Creator it is not good for him to be alone, that in the power of this saying a helper will be given him," he explains. "And the serious purpose of what makes the female, female is that she *is* this helper."[5] Neither male nor female is to be considered in isolation. What it means to be male does not make sense without taking the female into account. In the Genesis account, what it means to be female is defined with the male in view. For this reason, Barth is impatient with talk of "authentic" maleness or femaleness. "Authentic maleness and femaleness are both shameful things, in maintaining which the two can only sin against one another," he warns. "What may be gathered from Genesis 2:18 is that male and female belong to one another and are to be male and female in this belonging."[6] In other words, the two must not only be differentiated from one another, but also be taken together. We therefore learn what it means to be male and female by interacting with one another in the family and in the church.

A pressing question naturally faces us: is this male/female design important only in marriage, or does it have broader implications? It is certainly true that we find in the creation story the theological foundation upon which the practice of marriage is based. It establishes the boundaries within which sexual intercourse may appropriately take place. Sexual practice is legitimate only within the covenant union of a man and woman (Gen. 2:23–24). Jesus affirmed this in Matthew 19:4–9, noting that this is a creation pattern and not just a cultural one.

It was God's design from the beginning, and its alteration, even when it is permitted by God's law, can only be explained as accommodation to sinful disobedience (cf. Matt. 19:7–9). But the interdependence between male and female that Paul describes in 1 Corinthians 11:11–12 is not limited to those who happen to be married. Paul's emphasis on the interdependence of the sexes to the Corinthians indicates that it applies to the church as much as it does to the rest of society.

BEYOND SEXUAL EXPRESSION

Today's culture thinks about sex—a lot. And it does so primarily in terms of physical intimacy and sexual intercourse. For many, sex is synonymous with intimacy. A majority of American adults believe that one of the main reasons to have sex is to express intimacy with someone you love and to connect with another person in an enjoyable way.[7] At the same time, our culture does not believe that sexual activity should take place exclusively within the context of the marriage covenant. This is especially true of younger generations:

> Whereas practicing Christians still overwhelmingly tie sex to marriage, the move among the greater U.S. population—most evidently among younger generations—is a de-linking of marriage and sex. Sex has become less a function of procreation or an expression of intimacy and more of a personal experience. To have sex is increasingly seen as a pleasurable and important element in the journey toward self-fulfillment.[8]

Dale Kuehne notes that these trends are features of the extreme individualism, which marks what he calls the "iWorld." Kuehne explains, "Romantic relationships, intimacy, and sexuality are so connected in the iWorld that it is widely accepted that if you want to have genuine intimacy, then you need to have sex. Moreover, if you aren't in a sexual relationship, then many will assume you are lonely and unfulfilled."[9] In this way of thinking, intimacy is identical with sexual expression. This is the underlying assumption that shapes the debate about same-sex relationships. "As we have seen, the iWorld deconstructs gender and makes it less important relationally," Kuehne states. "What's paramount is that you find intimacy and fulfillment in your relationship."[10] It doesn't matter whether that intimacy is found with someone of the opposite sex or someone of the same sex. Since the experience is what matters most, our culture assumes, the context of the sexual experience is also unimportant. It may or may not be within the confines of a traditional marriage relationship.

Certainly, sexual expression is an important aspect of human experience and is one context in which we experience relational intimacy. The Bible has too much to say about sex, in terms of both guidelines and warnings, for us to think otherwise. But there is more to intimacy than sex. Kuehne points out that intimacy is not primarily a feeling produced by biochemical reactions in the brain but "a grace given to the soul."[11] Intimacy is not limited to the experience of two individuals who are seeking sexual gratification. The primary context in which we experience relational intimacy is within the framework of community. Relational intimacy is experienced first within the context of the family and then within the larger community of the church. The plethora of social clubs, civic organizations, and other gatherings in our culture are proof that the church is not the only place where relational intimacy may be found outside the family. But the church has something that these other groups do not. It is the dwelling of God through the Holy Spirit, and its members are agents of grace (Eph. 2:22; 1 Peter 4:10). The intimacy found there has a different quality and comes from a different source.

The importance of being male and female is not limited to the biology of reproduction or the experience of sexual intimacy. The New Testament's statements about male and female relationships in the congregation indicate that they have significance beyond the scope of the marriage relationship (see 1 Cor. 11:3–16; 1 Cor. 14:33–35; 1 Tim. 2:8–15; 1 Peter 3:1–7). Intimacy is more than sex, and the distinction between male and female matters outside the bedroom. Jonathan Grant warns that "to reduce sexuality to sex is to miss [its] deeper essence. The greater part of sexuality is affective or social, including our fundamental need for relational intimacy across a broad range of nurturing friendships," he explains. "There is, though, an important difference between 'desire for sex,' which is a physical urge, and 'sexual desire,' or *eros*, which covers a broad range of human longing, including our yearning to know our Creator."[12]

BROKEN CISTERNS
AND BROKEN HEARTS

The church has much to say about the boundaries for human sexuality but does not always offer much help to those who fall outside those boundaries. That's why some complain that the church's only prescription to those struggling with their sexuality is to pray. Similarly, when it comes to porn or other compulsive sexual behaviors, our main remedy is to "just say no." This approach implies that sexual preference and sexual practice are a matter of simple choice. Debate abounds regarding whether one's sexual preferences can be changed, but there should be no question that if they can be changed, they are not easily changed. As is the case with all illicit desires, there must come a point when we say no. But rarely is this ever a single act or decision. It is a habit of life and a matter of long, and sometimes painful, obedience.

In the last decade, evangelicals have become especially concerned about the growing acceptance of same-sex marriage. The majority of evangelicals were opposed to the United States Supreme Court's decision to legalize same-sex marriage in 2015. But evangelical concerns on this matter seem as focused on the question of religious liberty as they are on the question of morality. Meanwhile, those who support gay marriage wonder what all the fuss is about. Why not treat same-sex partnerships the same as traditional marriage, especially since they seem to provide the same kind of fulfillment for those involved?

The problems of sin and selfishness are not exclusive to homosexuality. Paul's denouncement of homosexuality in Romans 1:24–28 places it within a larger context of exchanging the truth of God for a lie. He depicts homosexuality as the culminating deviation of a culture that seeks to obtain from created things that which only God can provide. This is a world that has turned away from God and in on itself. The root problem of today's culture is not that it is "going gay." The problem of our culture is that it is in bondage to idolatry. It is following the downward spiral Paul describes in Romans 1. This is reflected in heterosexual practice as much as it is in homosexual practice. God's complaint about Israel voiced by the prophet Jeremiah well describes the problem of our age: "My people have committed two sins: They have forsaken me, the spring of living water, and have dug their own cisterns, broken cisterns that cannot hold water" (Jer. 2:13).

The fact that the experience of homosexual couples parallels those of heterosexual marriage does not validate such a union. The Bible's evaluation of homosexual practice is not based on the satisfaction or dissatisfaction of those who engage in it but on God's design. God is the one who has labeled homosexual practice sinful, impure, and immoral (Rom. 1:24–27; 1 Cor. 6:9). Many moderns chafe at such language. It seems harsh and unfeeling. They believe that the Bible's definition of sexuality is narrow and prejudiced. Even some Christians have found the Bible's strictures on these matters hard to swallow. Or they believe that such proscriptions are culturally bound and do not apply to today.

Jonathan Grant traces this objection to a shift in what many see as their basis of authority: "One of the most influential yet latent themes in contemporary Christianity that reflects the culture at large is the subconscious conviction that our lives are the 'primary text,' while Scripture plays the role of 'secondary text,' helping us to interpret and make sense of our personal experience."[13] In this approach, personal experience is the primary authority. We may look to Scripture for support and affirmation, but where there's a discrepancy, our own experience takes priority. Our feelings and experiences form the hermeneutical grid that we use to interpret biblical truth. Instead of submitting our lives and practices to Scripture, we submit Scripture to our lives and practices. Our personal desires become the final arbiter of what is ethical or acceptable.

"We see this most clearly in our sexual lives," Grant explains.[14] "Modern culture places sexual expression and orientation right at the heart of personal identity; 'authentic' sexuality has become our highest virtue and an irresistible prerogative. Yet ordering our sexual lives along these lines, even when we do consult Scripture as a guide, puts us at high risk of getting lost in the reinforcement loop of self-deception."[15] The desires of the human heart are not always a reliable guide. When the Scriptures are not our primary authoritative text, the heart is more liable to lead us astray than to direct us into truth. It is for good reason that Jeremiah 17:9 laments, "The heart is deceitful above all things and beyond cure. Who can understand it?"

SEXUALITY AND IDENTITY

How does sexuality shape identity? Today's culture says I am who I am based on my sexual attraction. If that attraction falls outside the bounds of what Scripture deems acceptable, then Scripture must be wrong. To deny that attraction is to deny who I truly am. Dale Kuehne observes, "The iWorld subjugates nature under identity, whereas the Bible asserts that identity develops out of nature. In the latter view, we begin with a given nature from which identity is constructed, maintained, sustained, or destroyed."[16] The Bible grounds human identity in a God-given sexual nature. The first salient fact revealed about humanity's creation in God's image in Genesis 1:27 is that we have been created male and female. The phrase "male and female" in this text is a biological rather than social or cultural distinction.[17] But the view of contemporary culture is that even biological identity can be self-determined. I can redefine my sex according to my personal perception. If I feel like a male or a female, then I am a male or a female, no matter what my biology says about me. I might even be a mixture of the two.

The difference between these two approaches is fundamental. In one, identity is self-constructed, and sexuality is malleable. In the other, identity is God given and begins with the biological differentiation of male or female. According to the modern view, we get to choose whether we want to be male or female. In the biblical view, we are *made* either male or female. The biological distinction between male and female also has social implications. According to theologian Stanley Grenz, the creation account of Genesis 2 points to our need for community: "As sexual beings, humans are fundamentally incomplete in themselves."[18] Further, "Human sexuality not only participates in this incompleteness but also spurs individuals to seek community through relationships."[19] In God's judgment it was not good for either the man or the woman to be alone. The fact that the woman was created for the man implies incompleteness on her part as much as it does on Adam's. But the creation of two complementary beings was not itself the solution to their need. God's intent was not merely to provide humanity with companionship and a means for reproduction but to reinforce to both that in themselves they were fundamentally incomplete. Sexual differentiation points to our more ultimate need to be in a relationship with God: "Viewed in this light, sexuality, understood as the sense of incompleteness and the corresponding drive for wholeness, forms the dynamic that not only seeks human relationships but also motivates the quest for God."[20]

The polarity of humanity's sexual nature also affects culture on a fundamental level in its two most important social institutions. First, it has implications for the family. Marriage, as the Bible defines it, is more than the mutual commitment of two people who love each other. The biblical idea of marriage is that it is a covenant union between a man and a woman. This is foundational to the nature of the family. Union between a man and woman is essential if marriage is to reflect humanity's God-given complementarity. Jesus affirmed this when He quoted the Genesis account in His discourse on marriage and divorce in Matthew 19:4–6: "'Haven't you read,' he replied, 'that at the beginning the Creator "made them male and female," and said, "For this reason a man will leave his father and mother and be united to his wife, and the two will become one flesh"? So they are no longer two, but one flesh. Therefore what God has joined together, let no one separate.'"

Marriage between a man and a woman is not a cultural invention. It is a divine institution. The same Creator who "made them male and female" also decreed that the two should be "one." It is God who has joined them together. Jesus is explicit about the sexual difference between those who enter into the marriage relationship. He says that marriage is between a man and his wife and mirrors the pattern of mother and father. Jesus also speaks implicitly of sexual differentiation when He states that the union of the two makes them one. This implies that apart they are something different from one another. The Bible knows of no paradigm for marriage other than the union of male and female. From a biblical perspective, the cultural label "same-sex marriage" is a self-contradiction.

The other foundational institution where humanity's sexual differentiation is important is the church. In fact, there is a connection between these two institutions. The structure of the family points to the higher order relationship between Christ and the church. The same words from Genesis 2:24, which Christ quotes in his discourse on marriage, are also quoted by Paul when he provides guidelines to Christian husbands. Paul, however, concludes with an important explanatory note: "This is a profound mystery—but I am talking about Christ and the church" (Eph. 5:32). When Paul calls the parallel between the marriage relationship with that of Christ and the church a "mystery," he is not saying that it is abstract or hard to fathom. In the New Testament, mystery is the language of revelation. A biblical mystery is a truth that was not previously understood but that which has now been made known by God. The family does not exist for its own sake. It does not exist merely to meet the social needs of society. The structure of the family actually points to the higher institution of the church.

Christ's role as the head of the church establishes a pattern for the two sexes in both domains. In the family, it places the husband in the role as the family's head (Eph. 5:23). Husbands are to love their wives sacrificially, just as Christ gave Himself for the church. The corollary command in Ephesians 5:22 telling wives to submit to their husbands poses a stumbling block for those who view submission through the lens of power. But the comparison to Christ is the key that removes this stumbling block. The responsibilities of biblical headship are love and sacrifice rather than control. The trajectory that mirrors Christ's relationship to the church is one that follows a path of descent (see Phil. 2:5–8). To be appointed to headship is to be called as a servant. Instead of creating a culture of spiritual feudalism, these defined roles are really an outworking of the mutual dependency that God established at creation. The role of the wife is that of peer, co-laborer, and strong helper in a mutually shared calling (Gen. 2:18). The obligation of the husband is to sacrifice himself on her behalf and recognize that the one that God has given him is "bone of my bones and flesh of my flesh" (Gen. 2:23).

Theologian Donald Bloesch characterizes the husband's authority as being "for" rather than "over" the other: "Subordination in the Pauline sense involves yielding to the love of the other, responding in love to the one who reaches out in loving embrace."[21] It is a matter of priority rather than hierarchy: "The Christian family is not a hierarchy in which the husband is over wife and children, nor a democracy in which the husband simply stands alongside wife and children and decisions are made on the basis of consensus: instead, it is a confraternity with levels of responsibility—the husband going *before* and *behind*, as one who leads and assists but does not dictate or try to control."[22]

Just as men and women have different roles in the family, so also they have different roles in the church. The New Testament speaks of gender-based distinctions in the church's public ministry and in its leadership structure. In 1 Corinthians 11:2–7, the apostle instructs those who engage in public prayer and prophecy in the assembly to behave differently according to gender. Women are to have their heads covered (perhaps a requirement to wear a veil or shawl), while men are to perform these same ministries with their heads uncovered. Paul's reasoning for this difference in vv. 8 and 9 is grounded in the Genesis account of creation. We do not know with certainty what form this covering took, but the essential point is clear: the difference between male and female is to be maintained, and it shapes interactions in the church even on the level of ministry. This is echoed further in the directives Paul gives in 1 Timothy 2:9–15, where gender-based restrictions are placed on the exercise of authority in the assembly.

Some contemporary readers are put off by these restrictions. They seem discriminatory and oppressive. But it is important to recognize that the New Testament church set limits on both genders. The Bible's perspective is not that women are the problem in the church and that men are better. The biblical perspective is that men and women both need the guidance of God's Word as they live in community. The other important point to bear in mind is that gender-based differences are a feature of every culture, even of those egalitarian cultures that decry them.

NEITHER MALE NOR FEMALE

How do we square these New Testament directives with Paul's assertion that in Christ there is neither male nor female (Gal. 3:28)? This verse cannot mean that biological differences between men and women suddenly disappear once someone becomes a Christian. Nor does it mean that the cultural distinctions between the two genders no longer affect our interactions with one another. Cultural perception of what is appropriately male or female played an important role in Paul's explanation of gendered behavior in the church (1 Cor. 11:6).

Paul tells us what he means in Galatians 3:26: "for in Christ Jesus you are all sons of God, through faith" (ESV). Paul is not talking about biological differences or even the fact that different rules guide behavior depending upon one's gender. He is talking about inclusion in the body of Christ. Jew and gentile, slave and free, male and female comprised the three major class distinctions of Paul's day. New Testament scholar F. F. Bruce observed, "It is not unlikely that Paul himself had been brought up to thank God that he was born a Jew and not a Gentile, a freeman and not a slave, a man and not a woman. If so, he takes up each of these three distinctions which had considerable importance in Judaism and affirms that in Christ they are all irrelevant."[23] The point is not that there are no differences between us who are in Christ. Paul's essential point is that in Christ there are no outsiders. Roles may differ, but status does not. No matter what distinctions separate people outside the church, all who are in Christ are members together of God's household. They are also members of one another.

The negatives in Galatians 3:28 do not render the ethnic, gender, or class differences that exist between us suddenly meaningless. They do not make us all androgynous or eliminate the social maze that we may have to navigate outside the church. They do establish a priority in our identity. Whatever else we may be in this world, we are in Christ first and foremost. It is this Christian identity that binds us together, even with those Christians who are unlike us.

Identity in Christ also changes the rules of interaction within the community of faith. The rules that apply outside the church may not be the same ones that apply within the church. In the New Testament church, slaves were accorded honor as brothers and sisters in Christ (Philem. 16). Women were given a voice through prayer and prophecy (1 Cor. 11:5). And James warned that in the assembly, the rich must not be shown special attention while the poor are dismissed (James 2:1–3).

It needs to be acknowledged, however, that our Christian identity does not guarantee a utopian experience when we come to church. Paul's directives about male and female roles in the assembly indicate that there was both disorder and deviation from accepted practice in Corinth (see 1 Cor. 11:16). His admonition to Philemon to receive Onesimus back as "a dear brother" suggests that Philemon may have struggled with seeing his former "useless" slave differently. And all the New Testament warnings about sexual practice and the dangers of sexual immorality make it abundantly clear that the church is a church on the ground. It wrestles with its identity and struggles with its practices.

In order to be truly biblical, a theology of manhood and womanhood must be balanced. Instead of focusing on what the Bible says about the relationship between men and women in the home and in the church, biblical conservatives sometimes give the impression that their argument is mostly with women. This one-dimensional perspective introduces an obsessive quality to the discussion that is unhealthy and ultimately unbiblical. Ignoring the distinctiveness of the sexes can lead to a distorted view of God's ideal for men and women, but an overemphasis on sexual distinctions can be just as damaging. The Bible affirms both the distinctiveness of the sexes and their mutual dependency. Placing too much emphasis on gender roles reduces biblical manhood and womanhood to a matter of function. Each is construed primarily in terms of what we do. To lead is to be a man. To follow is to be a woman. Men are initiators. Women are responders. The mark of true manhood is to "act like a man." The essence of womanhood is expressed only in the roles of wife and mother.

In *The Ethics of Sex*, theologian Helmut Thielicke writes that the totality of what it means to be human can be resolved into the two main dimensions of being and function. As *beings*, we relate to God, have incredible value, and are never to be used as a means to an end. As *functionaries*, we are capable of affecting the people and things around us. Thielicke warns of the enormously destructive potential of regarding sexuality merely as a function. When this happens, the importance of the person is lost. He explains, "One can actually state it as a formula that to the degree that this tendency to regard the person as a thing increases and the person is impugned at the point of his substantial being, men become stereotypes which are interchangeable at will."[24]

Thielicke is thinking of the erotic dimension of human sexuality. But his principle has a broader application. To define what it means to be a man or woman solely in terms of role is ultimately dehumanizing. Such a perspective is really a kind of utilitarianism that roots another's value in the service they provide to society and to the church. It degrades men and women to the status of mere "function-bearers." Thielicke warns, "To regard man merely as the bearer of a function, 'a functionary', is to dehumanize and make a thing of him, and therefore enslave him."[25] This is what pornography does when it reduces a person to a sex object. It is what the sweatshop does when it treats workers as if they were mere machines. And it is what we do when we say that the highest value of a man or woman comes from their particular role in the home or the church. Roles do exist and are important. Yet the value of the individual is not determined by one's role. Our value as individuals is intrinsic, determined by our relationship to God. We are not mere functionaries; we are human *beings* in fellowship with God and with one another.

One reason we dwell on gender roles so much is because the male voice predominates evangelical theology. The majority of those teaching and writing in the field are men. Yet scientific research has confirmed what common experience has shown us all along. Men and women are not the same. They perceive the world around them, process information, and approach relationships differently. In her book *Preaching That Speaks to Women*, Alice Matthews contrasts the "separate self," a typically male perspective, with the "relational self," which is often a female point of view. Someone who looks through the lens of the relational self sees relationships within a social context. "In contrast to the separate self, this self is defined in the context of social experience: I understand who I am (as a self) as I see your reaction to me—to my words and actions."[26] The perspective of the separate self sees the relationship through the lens of what that relationship provides. "For a person characterized by the separate self," Matthews explains, "relationships are *functional*."[27] This does not mean that women are friendlier than men. Nor does it mean that men are not interested in relationships. It does mean that men and women have different ways of relating and often value different things when it comes to relationships.

The truth of this difference in perspective was illustrated for me several years ago as I watched my son's soccer team. At the first practice of the season, the coach lined up the boys and started with a drill. Across the field, the girls' team was seated on the ground in a circle, learning the names of their team members. The boys' first order of business was functional. They were learning the basic skills of handling the ball. For the girls, the primary concern was knowing one another and building a sense of "team."

As a rule, biblical conservatives tend to view gender roles through the male lens of functionality. This has some value, but functionality is only one facet of what it means to be a man or woman. In order to see the complete picture, we need the theological perspective of both sexes. If it's true that men and women see the world differently, stifling the perspective of either sex will only lead to an inadequate theology. Adam's first mistake was his silence in the garden when Eve was being tempted. His subsequent error has been to silence the voice of his God-given partner.

HOW CULTURE
SHAPES OUR DEFINITIONS

Not long ago, a friend who is both a mother and a professional described the ambivalence she felt about the rhetoric often used to speak of the woman's role. "My children are grown and out of the house," she explained. "That dimension of my role is now a relatively small part of my life. So when I hear people say that a woman's 'highest calling' is to be a wife and mother, I find myself wondering if there isn't anything else for me to do for Christ."

There seems to be a double standard in such statements about women's roles. We often hear about the high calling of a wife and mother but rarely hear similar rhetoric used to speak of the male role, despite widespread evidence of the social damage caused by absent fathers. More importantly, we ought to ask if such an assumption is even accurate. The Bible does speak highly of a woman's role as wife and mother. But if these roles are a woman's *highest* calling, why doesn't Paul advise the unmarried women in Corinth to seek marriage (1 Cor. 7:28–35)? Why does he admonish those who have spouses to "live as if they do not" (1 Cor. 7:29)? When he counsels young widows to seek marriage in 1 Timothy 5:11–15, the reasons he gives are practical. He doesn't want young widows to be unnecessarily burdensome to the church. He doesn't want them to become idlers and gossips because they have too much time on their hands. Marriage and family are high callings and worthy of our energies. But the believer's highest calling is to be devoted to "the Lord's affairs" (1 Cor. 7:34).

Our ideas of what it means to be a man or woman are partly determined socially and may change over time and across cultures. Ideas of gender are learned nonverbally as we observe the behavior of men and women. These ideas are reinforced by the praise or sanction of society at large. As a result, our notion of gender often feels as if it's a matter of nature, when in reality it's learned and malleable. The answer to the question of what men and women should or should not do has changed, even in our own lifetime.

When I (John) was young, everyone assumed it was wrong for a boy to play with dolls. Then, someone came up with the idea of dressing a doll in army fatigues and giving it a weapon. Now, no boy would be ashamed of playing with a doll, as long as it is called an "action figure." Not too long ago, there were few options for girls and women in the realm of athletics. Most sports were considered to be a man's world. Today, there are professional leagues for women in many sports. Can a man wear a skirt and still be thought of as a man? He might, if he is from Samoa or if his name is Scottish and his skirt is called a *kilt*. Fifty years ago, a man who wore a gold earring would have been considered effeminate. Today, many see it as stylish.

We need to guard against the temptation to use the Bible to sanction customs that are merely social constructs. The Pharisees of Jesus' day tried to protect God's commands by putting a fence around the Law. I fear that we have gone beyond the Scriptures in our effort to preserve God's original design for gender roles. Have we added our own traditions to the list of what is commanded or forbidden in attempt to protect biblical manhood and womanhood? In Jesus' day, it was commonly understood that it was unfitting for women to study the Bible. Jesus ignored this cultural practice (Luke 10:39). Paul defied the same convention when he commanded the church to "let a woman learn" in 1 Timothy 2:11 (ESV). It is right to challenge cultural assumptions about gender roles when those assumptions are demeaning or destructive.

HONORING BOTH LOGOS AND ETHOS

Perhaps our greatest mistake in sorting out gender differences has been to emphasize logos and ignore ethos. We are understandably concerned about the Bible's doctrine of sexuality. We are less interested in the way we convey that truth or engage those who disagree with us. Our tone is acerbic, our posture combative, and our criticism one-sided. We do not limit ourselves to arguing against the theology we oppose; we attack the theologians. It could be argued that those with whom we disagree have been equally hostile towards us and that we are only answering in kind. While there may be plenty of guilt to go around, do we really believe that our ungracious words and unkind spirit can be justified simply by saying, "She hit me first?"

Throughout its history, the church has often struggled to be civil in its theological disputes. We've used harsh language and even come to blows. According to tradition, Bishop Nicholas of Myra slapped the heretic Arius across the face at the Council of Nicaea in AD 325. During the Reformation era, John Calvin titled one of his theological treatises "A Brief Reply in Refutation of the Calumnies of a Certain Worthless Person." Martin Luther was famous for his immoderate language when talking about his enemies. But the Bible prescribes a different approach to handling theological disputes. In 2 Timothy 2:24–26, Paul warns,

> the Lord's servant must not be quarrelsome but must be kind to everyone, able to teach, not resentful. Opponents must be gently instructed, in the hope that God will grant them repentance leading them to a knowledge of the truth, and that they will come to their senses and escape from the trap of the devil, who has taken them captive to do his will.

Before we condemn our opponents for not taking the clear teaching of Scripture seriously enough, let us take a dose of our own medicine and move the discussion to a higher level. It is not enough to be right. We must also be righteous.

MAKING PEACE IN THE CULTURE WAR

The world in which we live is hypersexualized and hypersensitive. It is sexually confused. Because of this, some believe the church should engage the culture and take back the institution of marriage. This is a culture-war approach. They urge believers to employ the same aggressive tactics and political savvy employed by those who have redefined traditional marriage. This posture is essentially adversarial. It is usually interpreted as hostility. The culture-war strategy also requires a level of organization and media presence that is beyond the reach of most churches. The typical congregation does not have the means or knowledge to mount a sophisticated media campaign supporting traditional marriage. If this is the only way the church can address the issue of sexual identity, then there is little the average Christian can do.

A major weakness of the culture-war approach is that it has little to offer those who are struggling with their sexuality. The *what* of human sexuality is clearly stated, but not the *how*. The result is a gospel without grace. The culture-war approach rightly condemns unbiblical practice but fails to offer a concrete way of escape or to model an alternative to those who may be convicted by its message. Its approach is overly simplistic, with a two-pronged message that is interpreted by those who hear it as "Just don't" and "Try harder."

The alternative to the culture-war approach is one that is relational. This strategy hopes to win the cultural battle through love and inclusion instead of the ballot box. It is a more winsome approach and one that seems more manageable. It's the kind of strategy a single congregation or an individual church member might employ. But this approach, too, is not without its challenges. The first and most obvious obstacle is one of connection. How do we establish meaningful relationships with those whose thinking and lifestyle are so different from our own? How do we persuade them that we are friendly? Most of all, how do we welcome them into our community without compromising our own convictions? The answer is that we must do it one person at a time.

Between these two strategies, it is the relational approach that is by far the most costly. It takes more time—years rather than months. And there is no guarantee that our efforts will yield results. A relational strategy is messier because it forces us to cope with our own discomfort as we attempt to move closer to those who are different from us and whose behavior may even be repulsive to us. This underscores the greatest differ-ence between these two approaches: the culture-war approach is about *positioning*; the relational approach is about *people*.

In her book *The Secret Thoughts of an Unlikely Convert*, former lesbian Rosaria Champagne Butterfield describes how an article she wrote for her local newspaper criticizing the Promise Keepers movement prompted a letter from a Presbyterian pastor in her community. In it, the pastor gently challenged her assumptions and invited her to begin a dialogue with him. When he subsequently invited her to his home for dinner, she accepted, thinking that the exchange would help her with the book she was writing about the Religious Right. What ensued instead was a long, life-transforming friendship with Pastor Ken and his wife, Floy.

As a result of their conversations, Butterfield began to read the Bible. As she did, doubts crept into her mind about her sexual identity and lifestyle. Then on one Sunday morning in February, she arose from the bed of her lesbian lover and went to church. Butterfield felt like a freak at first. Her conversion and her transformation were not immediate. It was a process that took years. During that time, Ken and Floy loved her with patience and continued to dialogue with her. The church prayed for her. And even when Butterfield finally began to follow Christ, she didn't suddenly stop feeling like a lesbian. In time, she began to see a difference. "Slowly but steadily, my feelings did start to change—feelings about myself as a woman and feelings about what sexuality really is and what it really isn't," Butterfield recalls. "I—like most everyone who identified as gay or lesbian—felt very comfortable, very at home in my body, in my lesbianism. One doesn't repent of a sin of identity in one session."[28]

During this journey, Butterfield felt welcomed by the church. "Did I find the perfect church?" Butterfield asks. "No. I almost left when things got hard, and they got hard fast. The time that I brought my drag queen friend to church pushed a lot of folks out of their comfort zone."[29] But each persisted in their own slow and imperfect way. The result was not a neat and orderly storybook conversion but one that Butterfield characterizes as a "train wreck." It upended her life and changed everything—her clothes, her job, even the way she talked and thought. None of this came without a struggle. Yet it was a true conversion. One with a transforming effect on all the parties involved.

This is the way forward for the church in a world that is both sexually obsessed and sexually confused. It is the way forward for a church afraid that it is on the losing end of the culture wars. It is the way of the gospel. It is the way of the cross. It is also the way of community. It does not begin with a program but with a person. Start with someone you know personally. This may be someone you know at work or even in your own family. Begin with relationship rather than rebuke. Employ the ordinary tools of social interaction to build a friendship. Ask them to tell you about their life. Invite them to dinner. Show them what your life really looks like. You do not need to be a perfect Christian. If the opportunity arises, introduce them to your community of believers. They do not need to be the perfect church. You do not need to have all the answers to their questions. You can accept them as a person without approving of their beliefs or behavior. Your role in all this is not to convince but merely to bear witness in deed and word. Conviction is the Holy Spirit's job. This is the path laid out for all Christian pilgrims by the loving hand of the God who has made us male and female.

IS UNITY POSSIBLE?

Is it possible to maintain unity in the church despite our differences—whether they are merely matters of opinion or our biological differences? The answer depends upon how we define *unity*. If by unity we mean unanimity in all our conclusions, the church's long experience offers ample proof that such an expectation is unrealistic. We disagree about many things. Some of our disagreements are profound. It seems likely that we will continue to disagree until we finally "attain[ ] to the whole measure of the fullness of Christ" (Eph. 4:13).

If unity means that we must never feel or express ourselves strongly about our differences, the answer must also be no. Not every difference between believers is worth shouting about, but there are many differences that merit passionate expression. It's possible to express strong disagreement and still act civilly toward one another. Disagreement is compatible with love. Indeed, it is often a mark of love. Disagreement isn't necessarily divisiveness. Our quest for biblical unity may be hindered by our tendency to define unity in emotional terms. We like to think of unity as a shared positive feeling. Anything that seems to disrupt that warm feeling is deemed a threat to unity. We also tend to confuse unity with uniformity. By this definition, anything that smacks of difference destroys unity.

The focus of biblical unity lies elsewhere. Biblical unity begins with a shared identity. We are a body made up of many members who have been joined to one another by the work of Christ and the Holy Spirit. This means the church's unity is a spiritual fact before it is an experience (John 17:20–23; Rom. 12:4–5; Eph. 2:22). Biblical unity is also a shared commitment to truth. More than a commitment to the general idea of truth, this is a firm commitment to a body of truth. It is a commitment to that collection of teachings the Bible characterizes as "the faith" (Acts 16:5).

Our commitment to these truths binds us together in our convictions. Such a commitment also distinguishes us from those who refuse to share those convictions. This is exactly what truth is supposed to do. According to Romans 16:17, the proper way to respond to those who claim to be followers of Jesus but reject the truth is to "keep away from them." What is more, the Bible's definition of what constitutes truth or "sound doctrine" involves more than theological abstractions like the doctrine of the Trinity. Doctrine also includes things like sexual practice (1 Cor. 5:11). This suggests that instead of ignoring our differences over sexual identity and practice, we ought to be examining them carefully.

Disagreements can greatly benefit the church. They provide a laboratory for learning the art of civil discourse. They teach us how we should and should not approach our differences. When they are focused on doctrines that matter, our disagreements also refine us by separating the wheat from the chaff.

Our disputes also help us to decide which matters are central and which are not. Not everything worth disagreeing about is worth fighting over. On the other hand, some things worth fighting over really are worth separating over. Might not God be using the confusion of our present cultural moment to help us understand what sex and sexuality have to do with being human and Christian? This conflict has forced the church to reexamine its own consistency and fidelity. It has also helped us to ask important questions about the expansiveness of God's welcome and the power of His grace. Just who does God accept? Does the gospel offer any real help to those who are struggling with their sexual identity or whose sexual desires fall outside the biblical norm?

Sexuality is a core component of the Bible's definition of human identity and experience. Humanity was created to be male and female. Sexual expression is more than a matter of either recreational enjoyment or animal desire. The presence of the Song of Solomon in the biblical canon—although it has at times made the church feel uncomfortable—implies that sexual desire and its expression are at least analogical of the deeper intimacy we experience with God. Philosopher Charles Taylor has observed that sexuality is a crucial aspect of bodily existence and making theological sense of it in a secular age will inevitably force the church to reexamine its sexual ethics. "But it demands more than this," Taylor observes. "We have to recover a sense of the link between erotic desire and the love of God, which lies deep in the Biblical traditions, whether Jewish or Christian, and find new ways of giving expression to this."[30] What we experience as conflict, cultural confusion, and threat may actually be a kind of signpost meant to point us to God, albeit by unexpected and unlikely paths.

God sometimes uses the church's disagreements to sort true "believers" from those who merely profess faith (1 John 2:19). We're not supposed to agree with everyone simply because they claim to be a Christian. Wolves lurk among the flock (Acts 20:28–30), and goats mingle with the sheep (Matt. 25:31–46). The church also includes the misguided, who are genuinely sincere but are sincerely wrong. Yet there is some room for common ground even for those who share significant differences about sexual practice and identity.

For one thing, we can all agree that God is deeply interested in those whose views and practices fall outside the cultural or biblical norm. We can affirm the pain and acknowledge the scars of those who have struggled with their sexual identity or their sexual practice. We can agree that God extends His love to those who have violated His design for human sexuality. We can hold out the hope of God's forgiveness and transforming grace offered to all who turn to Jesus Christ in genuine faith. What we cannot do is say that our differences on these issues do not matter. We must not succumb to the tranquilizing effect of postmodern ambiguity. Nor should we settle for an anemic version of church unity that forces us to minimize our profound differences and leave them unaddressed simply because those differences make us uncomfortable. Our differences are not always reconcilable. By all means, let us continue the debate. But let us first lay down our weapons.

Questions for Reflection

1. Why do you think issues of sex and gender are such a concern for our culture? What should the church's main message be regarding sexual identity?

2. How would you respond to someone who says that Christians are old-fashioned and narrow-minded when it comes to sexuality and traditional marriage?

3. Many conflicts in the church are based on differences between men and women regarding leadership. What difference does it make to the church that God created humanity to be male and female?

4. How should churches respond to laws that run against what the Bible teaches regarding marriage and sexuality?

5. Is it possible for a church to welcome those who disagree with the Bible's teaching on sexuality without compromising its stand on these issues? What might this look like?

8

GENERATIONAL DIFFERENCES

Drew is part of a demographic revolution. He is a millennial who serves on the management team of a big-box retail store, and older employees often report to him. The dynamic is sometimes awkward, especially in his minimum-wage setting. "Most Boomers you find in retail are not in upper management. They aren't on 'Plan A.' They aren't even on 'Plan B,'" he observes. "They've been exiled by circumstance to the far reaches of the alphabet and sometimes all the way back around again."

Drew acknowledges that generational differences exist but is wary of making too many generalizations about them. "In my experience, all the talk of Men-are-from-Mars-Women-are-from-Venus-style generational personality clashes are a bunch of mumbo jumbo," he says. "I believe that most conflicts that occur on account of generational lines are a result of changes in language and custom that simply make effective connection between people difficult."

Yet Drew believes that age matters. "If someone is older

than you, they know more than you. Period. It doesn't mean they are always right and you're always wrong. But it does mean that they have seen some things that you haven't. Listen carefully when someone older than you speaks. You might learn something."

Where there is a generational gap, Drew believes it is his responsibility to make the first move to close it. "Find a way to meet people where they are already at and take them with you. Don't expect them to just get on your level. If there is a connection gap, it's up to you to find common ground and begin moving forward."

Depending on where you draw the lines between generations, as many as five generations could be sharing leadership responsibilities in churches today. Figuring out who fits where is not as easy as you might think. It is certainly not a calculation that can be made with scientific precision, because generational differences are more a matter of perception than biology. To some degree, they are a fiction of social identity, labels that have been imposed on one group by another, occasionally to the chagrin of those who are assigned them. While there are always exceptions among individuals, each collective generation does seem to have certain characteristics that set it apart from the others.

News anchor Tom Brokaw dubbed the men and women who came of age during World War II and the Korean War "the greatest generation," while others called them "the silent generation." Born between 1901 and 1945, these were the traditionalists who argued with their children about the Vietnam War and coined the phrase "generation gap." Although there are still some of this generation present in our churches, they are no longer a large leadership presence. They have been replaced by the boomers (1946–1964), the iconoclasts of the Woodstock generation and the original members of the Jesus Movement. The boomers grew up, got jobs, are now growing grey and starting to cash in their retirement accounts. They still wear blue jeans, but their revolutionary fervor has largely died down. In some ways, boomers have become the establishment they used to rail against.

After the boomers come the "slackers" of Generation X (1965–1980). Dubbed the lost generation by some, Generation X is seen as skeptical, pragmatic, and organizationally detached. Viewed more positively, they tend to be flexible, practical, and independent. According to Ed Stetzer, while boomers tend to ask "Is it right?" those who came after them ask "Is it fair?"[1] A smaller cohort than boomers and millennials, Xers can feel overlooked and invisible. However, by 2028, they will outnumber boomers by almost a million. For the present, Generation X interests tend to be overshadowed by the generational narcissism of baby boomers and cultural infatuation with millennials. More family-oriented than their boomer parents, Generation X prefers to maintain a balance between work and the rest of life. They are more comfortable with Google culture than traditional corporate culture and prefer to work independently instead of in groups.

Following on the heels of Generation X are the more optimistic millennials (or Generation Y), a generation that was born between 1981 and 2000, who were nurtured by helicopter parents and who learned to expect a trophy just for showing up. Millennials have many values in common with Generation X. Like the generation that preceded them, they are comfortable with technology. They share Xers' appreciation of balance in work and life but tend to be more comfortable working in groups than independently. They value mentoring and hunger for affirmation from their elders. Millennial optimism makes them adventurous. While boomers have a penchant for crafting vision statements, millennials are more inclined toward entrepreneurial action.

Although it is a little early to see the full shape that the rising generation of postmillennials or Generation Z (those born after 2000) will take in the life of the church, some differences are already beginning to surface. Generation Z seems to be the most comfortable with cultural diversity of any preceding generation. Barack Obama, the first African American president of the United States and the first to be biracial, is also the first president they are likely to remember. During their adolescence, the fight over bathroom access for the transgendered made headlines. Generation Z tends to be flexible in their thinking about gender roles and has come of age in a culture that has begun to view gender identity as a matter of self-selection as much as biology. For this reason, some suggest that they should be called the Pluralist Generation.[2] They are the most digitally embedded of all the generations. Like the millennials that preceded them, Generation Z is drawn to entrepreneurialism and idealism. They are likely to be pioneers and adventurers. It remains to be seen whether they will have the patience to persevere through the mundane struggles of the church. This is the generation that fills the church's youth groups and has begun to make its way into college. Generation Z is still a little too young to be concerned about what it means to share power with boomers, Xers, and millennials in the church, but they are starting to filter into the workplace. Soon they won't be the focus of the church's youth ministry any longer. They will be the ones doing the ministry.

WHEN GENERATIONS GIVE WAY

Age is a major factor in identity. When we are in our sixties, we do not see ourselves the same way we did when we were in our twenties. Age also affects the way we view others. A famous saying often attributed to Mark Twain observes, "When I was a boy of fourteen, my father was so ignorant I could hardly stand to have the old man around. But when I got to be twenty-one, I was astonished at how much he had learned in seven years."

Like the workplace, the church is experiencing a major demographic transition as boomers, Xers, millennials, and Generation Z learn how to live and lead together. Their collaboration has the potential to enrich the church, but this blessing will not come automatically. At present, collaboration is proving to be something of a battleground, as one generation vies with another and each attempts to navigate the others' differences in experience, outlook, and expectations. Ecclesiastes 1:4 declares, "Generations come and generations go, but the earth remains forever." In reality, it works the other way around, at least according to the word order in the Hebrew text. One generation goes before the next generation comes. But for a time, each must dwell together. They do not always find it easy sharing power.

Generational labels change, but the challenge is the same. It's always difficult for one generation to give way to another. Paul urged Timothy, "Don't let anyone look down on you because you are young, but set an example for the believers in speech, in conduct, in love, in faith and in purity" (1 Tim. 4:12).

Churches are trying to come to terms with the conflicting values and styles of each generation. The handoff of leadership responsibility is often difficult, with the older generation clinging to position and power. In their youth, boomers were famous for being innovationists and iconoclasts. Their impatience toward the preceding generation was summed up by these Bob Dylan lyrics:

> *Your old road is rapidly aging.*
> *Please get out of the new one*
> *If you can't lend your hand,*
> *For the times they are a-changin'.*

Boomers who once raised a defiant fist at the establishment *are* the establishment now and find it hard to share power with Xers and millennials, even when they invite them to the table. Carson Nyquist, coauthor of *The Post-Church Christian*—a book about intergenerational tension coauthored with his boomer father, Paul—notes that those who want to lead often need to create their own opportunities. "I think it's fair to say few of us have the opportunity to lead Boomers," Nyquist observes. "If anything, I see ambitious Millennials creating space to gain experience leading, yet often this does not include Boomers below or beside them. My sense is that both generations feel awkward about Millennials taking leadership when Boomers are involved." According to Nyquist, boomers are more inclined to remain in their position or simply retire than they are to share leadership with subsequent generations. "Rarely have I seen a Boomer empower a Millennial and then stick around on the team," he states.[3]

Jonathan's first ministry assignment was serving the youth in a church led by boomers. Although he was given the title "leader," he didn't always feel trusted or respected. "At times it felt almost like playing church," he observes. "It's like playing house when you were younger. You think you are doing something real at grandma's house, but all that really happened is she patted you on the head in affirmation of your youthful dreaming." Sarah's leadership experience has been similar. "I've really loved working with Boomers in the few times I've had the opportunity to lead them. But it has usually tended to have a really paternal feel," she explains. "Even when they're following me, it's in a 'look at you go!' sort of way." Sarah finds that she usually has to "lead from below" with boomers, even when her title implies that she is the one with more authority. She finds that boomers often dismiss the ideas proposed by younger leaders. She has learned to work in this environment but feels that it limits her ability to lead. "There are some issues that I cannot address because I won't be taken seriously," she says.

These complaints seem to reflect disappointment more than anger. Younger leaders do not necessarily want to replace boomers or even rule over them. They are simply looking for an opportunity to lead alongside.

OPEN-OFFICE LEADERSHIP

Generational differences are reflected in leadership style. Mark Aardsma launched three companies while he was in his twenties and now works as a business coach with other entrepreneurs. Most of his clients are millennials. He thinks Xers and millennials are uncomfortable with a style of leadership that emphasizes chain of command. "I don't think people my age like to be bossed around," he notes. His companies have standards and expectations. There is an authority structure. But, as Mark puts it, "there is not a lot of command and control."[4] This is typical of post-boomers who are comfortable challenging leadership hierarchy. It was also typical of boomers before they reached the top of the hierarchy.

The approach to leadership favored by both Xers and millennials might be best described as egalitarian and situational. It is a style not especially bothered about titles. A popular saying declares, "When the student is ready, the teacher will appear." Generation X and millennial leadership could be characterized similarly: "When the need arises, the leader will appear." These generations are most comfortable with a fluid environment where the leadership task is shared and everyone's voice has weight.

Kerwin Rodriguez, a millennial who serves on the pastoral faculty of Moody Bible Institute, uses an architectural analogy to describe the approach of Xers and millennials. "Think open-office architecture applied to leadership," he says. This approach is more about influence and less about position. It is also an approach that requires humility. "Don't think about the glory or credit," Rodriguez urges. "The value is less about you getting recognition and more about the group succeeding. When the team wins, you win. If you win but the team loses, that's an utter failure." As an ethnic minority, Rodriguez believes his experience as a Hispanic working in a predominately Anglo culture has helped him. "I've already been conditioned for some of the obstacles. You have to learn how to play well with others."[5]

While they are generally egalitarian in their approach,

Xers and Millennials do have some differences in leadership style. Generation-X leaders are comfortable with compromise but tend toward independent decision-making after taking multiple views, which are usually given in private, into account. Millennials prefer to work through issues collaboratively. Both employ a "low power" approach to leadership and neither is especially impressed with titles. But their decision-making process can be very different. Generation X and millennials are egalitarian in the sense that they are comfortable having multiple voices weigh in on a decision regardless of their role or title. But where they differ is in how, and by whom, the final decision is made.

The difference between these two approaches is mainly one of emphasis. For Generation X, the stress is on the importance of hearing. For the millennial, it is upon the importance of being heard. Both allow multiple voices to speak into an issue, but because the Generation-X leader is most comfortable with independent action, he or she is likely to make the decision after people have expressed themselves in private. One study observed, "Individuals of Generation X aim to achieve and plan behavior rather than react spontaneously, and they are more willing to withdraw in order to find a solution that is acceptable to all (or to simply avoid the confrontation). They are more adrift and pleasant."[6] Remember, these were the latchkey kids who let themselves into the house while their parents were at work and amused themselves by playing video games. For them, holding a group meeting in which everyone shares their complaints or differences isn't necessarily productive. Or if there is such a meeting, the Generation-X leader may prefer to issue a directive after taking into account what has been said.

The team orientation of millennials places more weight

on the process of deliberation. For the millennial, simply being able to express yourself is not satisfactory. You must also have a sense that someone is listening. Millennials are more open to risk and more comfortable with conflict than Generation X. However, millennials are also the least empowered of the three. They see themselves as a generation waiting in the wings for their turn. And the leveling approach of Xers and millennials can be misinterpreted by boomers as an absence of settled convictions. They find it hard to take direction from leaders who are the same age as their children.

Even though they aren't impressed with titles or credentials, those of younger generations leading boomers need to own their leadership responsibility. This means that younger leaders will need to acquire leadership skills that may be outside their comfort zone. Aardsma explains, "When leading people who are older than oneself, there is definitely a need to embrace the fact that you are the leader even though you are younger. Don't abdicate or defer. If you are leading those who are used to structure and you are a soft leader, step up and fill the shoes. It's position not age that makes you a leader."[7]

DIFFERENT ANGLES OF VISION

The differences between millennials, Xers, and boomers provide a healthy balance of perspectives. Yet these same differences are just as liable to lead to crossed signals. Boomers seem to favor a problem-oriented approach. The benefit of age and experience has given them a keen eye for anticipating threats and potential obstacles. Xers are skeptical and independent in their decision-making. They're suspicious of pat answers and programmed solutions. This angle of vision sets the stage for critical thinking. Xer detachment positions them for flexibility in finding solutions to problems. The Xer preference for independent action makes them quick to take initiative and willing to work hard once they have committed to a course of action. Millennials tend toward optimism and collaboration. They favor a deliberative process and are quick to offer ideas. Their optimism offers a healthy contrast to boomer pessimism and Xer cynicism.

The SWOT analysis is emblematic of these differences, where leadership vision grows out of a careful analysis of Strengths, Weaknesses, Opportunities, and Threats. When boomers scan the SWOT landscape, their attention is drawn to the obstacles and threats standing in the way. Millennials, who have been characterized as "America's most stubborn optimists," would rather dwell on strengths and opportunities.[8] According to Paul Taylor, "They have a self-confidence born of coddling parents and everyone-gets-a-trophy coaches. They have a look-at-me élan that comes from being humankind's first generation of digital natives (before them, nobody knew that the whole world wanted to see your funny cat photos). And they have the invincibility of youth."[9] Meanwhile, Xer skepticism makes them suspicious of the entire exercise. Impatient with boomer minesweeping and the chirping optimism of millennials, Xers would just as soon skip the meeting and try to address the problem on their own.

The optimistic collaboration of millennials provides a needed counterbalance to boomer realism and Xer independence. Xer skepticism weans the church away from its simplistic formulas and stock answers. Meanwhile, boomer realism has the potential to help the other two generations discern the difference between cynicism, naïve optimism, and genuine faith. Boomer realism points to the way of wisdom. The critical thinking of Xers points to the way of truth. The optimism of millennials points toward the way of faith. All these differences are essential in the church and can lead to greater unity.

However, the presence of complementary perspectives is not a guarantee that we will benefit from them. The fact that we *are* all together does not necessarily mean that we will all *work* together. These generational differences have created fault lines in the relational landscape. Boomers, Xers, and millennials all feel a measure of frustration about their place in the church. Boomers are feeling more and more that their interests are being ignored and that their place in the church is becoming more marginal. As D'Vera Cohn and Paul Taylor observe in a Pew Research report, "This famously huge cohort of Americans finds itself in a funk as it approaches old age."[10] This might come as a surprise, given their numbers. It certainly does not seem to square with complaints by Xers and millennials who say they have difficulties finding leadership opportunities.

In some respects, boomer discontent may be more a problem of perception than of power. Boomers are used to being in charge. The product of the post–World War II population explosion, they are most comfortable being at the center. Boomers have enjoyed majority status most of their lives. This generation, which has been demographically described as the "pig in the python," is still king of the hill. Boomers possess the lion's share of wealth and hold most of the positions of power. But these days, they're feeling encroached upon and threatened. Some of this may simply be the unfortunate legacy of a generation that has spent most of its life being famous for being young. But some of the discomfort is sparked by a sense of displacement. The church's focus on the young is not a new trend. To a great extent, in fact, it is a mindset that was fostered by the boomers themselves. Now that they have discovered that they were unable to stay "forever young," boomers are feeling invisible and neglected. They have begun to question whether they are valued. In some cases, they feel used, and in others, obsolete.

Because of this, Jerell Carper, pastor of youth ministries at Antioch Church in Bend, Oregon, advises millennials who interact with boomers to listen well. "Mine wisdom from their unique perspective and value their generational differences," Carper explains. This is an attitude that reflects vulnerability, affirmation, and respect. "I need to show vulnerability by admitting that I don't know everything and I'd love any and all insight they give. Affirm that they still have so much to offer the body of Christ and the world. Ask them to share ways they've used their gifts or felt excluded. Show active listening skills."[11]

Ironically, Xers may have even more cause than boomers to feel marginalized. It's common today to find corporations, educational institutions, and churches led by boomers stressing about how to attract, accommodate, and assimilate millennials. Few did this for Generation X, which has been labeled the invisible generation, perhaps because it rarely makes demands the way boomers and millennials sometimes do. Xers do not define themselves as sharply as other generations. Their social location has produced a generation whose perspective is more of a blend between the two that bookend it. For this reason, we might think of Generation X as the "Bridge" Generation. Its experiences give it the unique capacity to grasp the thinking of the other two generations. Xer ambivalence positions it to play a key mediator role as boomers struggle with the handoff to subsequent generations. What looks like invisibility or a lack of conviction may actually be a kind of humility. As Paul Taylor observes about those in Generation X, "From everything we know about them, they're savvy, skeptical and self-reliant; they're not into preening or pampering, and they just might not give much of a hoot what others think of them. Or whether others think of them at all."[12]

GENERATIONAL ISSUES
IN THE ETHNIC CHURCH

For ethnically homogenous churches, specifically for congregations whose culture has been shaped by first-generation immigrants, generational identity includes an added layer of challenge. Not only does the older generation of leaders have difficulty letting go of power, the second generation is drawn to a style of church with a more Americanized culture. The hierarchical leadership style of many Asian immigrant churches is rooted in a tradition of loyalty and respect for age but is at odds with the individualism and youth orientation of American culture. This creates tension for second-generation members, whose style tends to be more democratic and collaborative than the leadership culture of their elders. Yet traditional Asian values have also inspired some second-generation Asian believers to create a leadership culture that unites the best of both worlds. "In fashioning their own unique expressions of spirituality, the younger ministers feel that several elements of immigrant spirituality need to be preserved and practiced within their newly formed churches," Timothy Tseng explains.[13] "Most importantly, many believe that immigrants better understand and practice the key Biblical concept of community because they come from a Confucian society that stresses the importance of the collective over the individual."[14]

This bicultural angle of vision is producing an approach to leadership that combines the strengths of both Asian and American culture. It downplays the distinction between clergy and laity in favor of the priesthood of all believers. This new generation understands the important place that relationships have in leading. Instead of expecting respect simply because a leader bears the title of pastor, they believe the pastor earns the respect of the congregation by caring for the flock (1 Peter 5:2–3).

Like the Asian church, Hispanic and Latino churches are also struggling to hold on to second-generation youth, and for many of the same reasons. Their overall congregational demographic is young, but congregations lack the resources for age-specialized ministries targeting youth. "Given the competing demands on Latino pastors, little time and energy can be dedicated to ministries that specifically target youth," one study produced by the Center for the Study of Latino Religion observes.[15] "Hispanic churches of all denominations report difficulties in retaining the second generation and attracting young people to ministry."[16] Generational differences over language and the degree to which each age group has adopted American culture are partly to blame, as is a clergy-centered approach that does not cast a vision for lay involvement or intergenerational leadership. Julio Guarneri, pastor of Calvary Baptist Church in McAllen, Texas, notes that one of the greatest sources of conflict in Hispanic churches is due to a lack of awareness of cross-cultural dynamics. "Often church people assume that, because they share the label 'Hispanic' or because they speak Spanish or because they share similar last names, they have the same culture," Guarneri explains.[17] "Some first generation pastors who come from various parts of Latin America assume they are coming to minister in the same cultural context."[18]

Guarno warns that this lack of awareness lends itself to spiritualizing problems that result from cultural misunderstanding. He recommends an approach combining spiritual sensitivity with cultural intelligence. "One of the best things we can do, regardless of our cultural background, is to be keenly aware of our own, to respect the way others do things, to ask questions with a teachable spirit, and to request feedback from others. Seek the Spirit to help you sort out the difference between biblical convictions and cultural norms."[19] It's evident that church leaders must learn to think like missionaries when the congregation is culturally diverse. Guarno warns that we need to think like a missionary even when everyone in the congregation shares the same ethnic label. "Whether you are a first-, second-, or third-generation Hispanic and whatever the country of your ancestry might be, if you minister in the U.S., you need to see yourself as a cross-cultural missionary. Rather than expecting people to adopt your culture, a good missionary adopts the culture of the people he/she seeks to reach."[20]

Generational tension also affects the African American church, but in different ways. In general, African Americans attend church more frequently than white Americans, and a "significantly higher" percentage of African Americans pray every day in comparison to the general population. According to the Pew Research Center, "African-Americans are more likely to be affiliated with a faith compared with the public overall, but as with the general population, younger African-Americans are more likely than their older counterparts to report being unaffiliated with a religion. For example, nearly one-in-five African-Americans under age 30 (19%) are unaffiliated, compared with just 7% of African-Americans who are age 65 and older."[21] Research suggests that older blacks are more involved in church than younger blacks.[22] The generational divide in the African American church is especially pronounced among young urban males. Larry Mamiya notes, "According to some observers, the studies on African American youth do not deal with the depth of alienation from black churches and mainstream culture that some young people feel."[23] And "many rap songs and hip hop culture speak of the 'nihilism' among black urban youth."[24]

The age of pastors in African American churches skews slightly older than white clergy. In his summary of research on trends in the black church, Mamiya observes that these leaders stay in place longer for financial reasons. "As we pointed out in 1990, the continued lack of pension and retirement benefits, 'compounds the age and generational problems of succession in these denominations when black clergy must continue to work long past retirement age in order to survive economically.'"[25] With the exception of a handful of large megachurches, black clergy earn less than white clergy and are not provided with housing benefits.

Overall, the American church is having difficulty transferring leadership from one generation to another. In the past twenty-five years, the average age of senior pastors has increased by a decade from forty-four to fifty-four. In 1968, nearly half of all clergy were under the age of forty-five. Today, only one in seven is under the age of forty. This age gap is all the more striking considering that most pastors get their sense of calling while they're still in their teens.[26] David Kinnaman, president of the Barna Research Group, posits several reasons for this. Increased life expectancy, economic necessity, the failure of churches to effectively develop younger leaders and implement succession planning, and the allure of other more entrepreneurial alternatives for Generation X and millennials may all be factors. Pastors also are staying in place longer. Twenty-five years ago, the average tenure of a pastor was only four years. Today, it is a decade. "It's not inherently a problem that there are older pastors in positions of leadership," Kinnaman explains.[27] "In fact, younger generations are often looking for wisdom and leadership from established teachers and leaders. The problem arises when today's pastors do not represent a healthy mix of young, middle age and older leaders. For the Christian community to be at its best, it needs intergenerational leaders to move it forward."[28]

THE SECRET TO LIFE TOGETHER

The church's generational differences have the potential to produce a community whose strengths complement one another, but they can also divide us. The benefits of intergenerational community do not come without a cost. Every generation values community, but we all do not agree on what true community looks like.

The boomer notion of community is local and sometimes even spatial. Even though they know that the church is not the building, when they think of church, they think of the place where the church meets. This should come as no surprise. Many boomers spent their formative years in a church environment where community was primarily a matter of showing up. Serious Christians attended church every Sunday morning. The truly serious attended Sunday night service as well. The spiritual elite showed up for Wednesday night Bible study and prayer. Those days have long since passed for most churches. What remains is a vision of congregational life that defines community primarily as commitment. The old formula has changed. Boomer pastors chide those who show up only for worship. They claim that the truly serious "get involved" in a small group. The spiritual elite host the group in their homes and engage in service projects together or participate in short-term missions.

Xers, though comfortable standing aloof, also recognize the importance of community. However, they are probably more inclined to see it epitomized in their own family experience. Many had children later in life than their parents, and their approach to parenting is shaped by a reaction to the isolation of their latchkey experience. Family is more important to Xers than the formal meetings of the church. Xer skepticism (sometimes viewed as cynicism by boomers) makes them sensitive to the hyperbole that the church often uses to describe its experience of community. They do not automatically associate the idea of community with the institution. "Most Gen Xers really do care about the world around them. We want to live lives of purpose. We want to inhabit communities that flourish," Andrew Thompson, a Gen-X leader in the United Methodist Church explains.[29] "And so, unwilling to buy into either a big-institution mentality or a save-the-world idealism, our usual tack is to focus on our own local contexts. In the church, that local focus means the congregation and the congregation's immediate environment."[30]

Millennials, on the other hand, define community as intimacy among peers, and they feel that authenticity is the primary means of creating relational capital, says Sam Hannum, a millennial who serves with Merge Community Church in Westland, Michigan. Boomers see community as a matter of relational standing between co-inhabitants who exist within a particular community. Hannum believes both approaches are valuable: "Boomers are very good at not invading your space both relationally and physically, yet Millennials crave relational interaction. On the other hand, Millennials have a vibrancy which I think many Boomers applaud and desire, yet that same vibrancy, unbridled without regard for structure, pushes many Boomers away."[31]

The millennial idea of community is marked more by the quality of the experience than by a commitment to a particular group. Community is defined as authenticity. Yet when asked to describe what this looks like, they often find it hard to put into words and typically offer vague synonyms instead. To be authentic is to be genuine. Authentic community is a community where people can be real. Authentic people are transparent. The ideal community, according to millennials, is one where believers are accepted just as they are, warts and all. When asked how this differs from the boomer notion of community, one millennial college student contrasted it with his family experience. "My father is a good guy," he said. "But all he ever talks with me about are cars. He's never told me about his struggles."

Another suggested that millennial talk about authenticity

is really a euphemism for spiritual struggle. "We are not really being authentic when we talk about authenticity," he said. "What we should really call it is sin." What seems to be in view here is a vision of a life together that is unaffected and characterized by a radical commitment to acceptance without judgment. This can look like indifference or even compromise to boomers, especially when it is demonstrated by those in leadership. In turn, boomer reserve is interpreted by millennials as hypocrisy.

What, then, is the secret to creating a multigenerational community that values one another and shares in the task of leadership? It begins with the recognition that our mutual strengths are also our greatest weaknesses. The things we see most clearly will blind us to the angle of vision that others provide. The unique perspective that each generation brings to the table strengthens the church but also blinds us to the contributions of those not like us. This means that true multi-generational community brings with it a significant measure of shared discomfort. We will not immediately appreciate the gift that others bring to the community. Our initial response to their interests, ideas, and aspirations is more likely to be irritation than inspiration.

Ironically, it is not a boomer, Xer, or a millennial whose counsel shows us the way forward and can help us heal the present divide. Rather, it comes from someone who learned the art of Christian community during the rigors of World War II. In his classic treatise on the nature of Christian community entitled *Life Together*, Dietrich Bonhoeffer emphasizes the importance that people, place, and a realistic sense of our own sinfulness have for community. He observes, "The physical presence of other Christians is a source of incomparable joy and strength to the believer."[32] Community requires commitment to a particular people in a specific place. Virtual community, therefore, is an oxymoron. Bonhoeffer also speaks frankly about the need for realism—or what many today would call authenticity. "The serious Christian, set down for the first time in a Christian community, is likely to bring with him a very definite idea of what Christian life together should be and to try to realize it," Bonhoeffer cautions.[33] "But God's grace speedily shatters such dreams. Just as surely as God desires to lead us to a knowledge of genuine Christian fellowship, so surely must we be overwhelmed by a great disillusionment with others, with Christians in general, and, if we are fortunate, with ourselves."[34]

The key to successful community under such conditions is not a specific organizational structure or particular leadership style but a set of virtues. Specifically, it demands we become practiced in the three deferential virtues: showing preference for others, intentional self-denial, and gracious withdrawal. Paul calls believers to show preference for others in Philippians 2:3 when he urges, "Do nothing from selfish ambition or vain conceit, but in humility regard others as better than yourselves" (NRSV). This counsel sounds strange to those who come from a culture obsessed with the importance of self-esteem. But to consider others "better" does not necessarily mean that we think poorly of ourselves. It means that we will give others preference. We will put them first. To consider others "better" is the opposite of selfish ambition (v. 3). Paul offers a snapshot of what this virtue looks like in action in 2:4: "Let each of you look not to your own interests, but to the interests of others." We show preference for others by studying their interests. But because we do not necessarily share those interests, showing preference is often coupled with a second deferential virtue. Those who show preference also practice self-denial.

Allowing the interests of others to guide my actions often calls me to sublimate my own. The tension we experience in a multigenerational community comes from the recognition that not everyone can have their way. Whose preferences will hold sway? Self-interest predisposes us to answer this question competitively. All-or-nothing thinking tells us it is either us or them. Certainly, there will be times when this will be the case, but that is not exactly what Paul says here. The admonition is to look out for the interests of others as well as our own. Generational differences are not always comfortable, but they are often complementary. Showing preference for the interests of others is often the best way to look out for my own.

But the primary deferential virtue where intergenerational differences are concerned is the intentional practice of gracious withdrawal. In the end, the author of Ecclesiastes is right. One generation gives way to another (Eccl. 1:4). Giving way is not only the natural trajectory of generations; in many respects, it is our obligation. This was both the assumption and the necessity that caused Paul to make Timothy his protégé and then later write to him: "You then, my son, be strong in the grace that is in Christ Jesus. And the things you have heard me say in the presence of many witnesses entrust to reliable people who will also be qualified to teach others" (2 Tim. 2:1–2). The connection Paul made between grace and this intergenerational responsibility was no accident. Grace is not only the *goal*, it is the *means* by which these things are accomplished.

If Bonhoeffer is right when he says that disillusionment is the first step toward genuine Christian fellowship, then our generational differences are not obstacles to community but are the grist from which authentic community is made. It is not a constructed atmosphere or our particular tastes that create community. There is no foundation for community other than the one that has already been laid. It is our bond in Jesus Christ that is the ultimate basis for life together. Bonhoeffer is right: "Christianity means community through Jesus Christ and in Jesus Christ. No Christian community is more or less than this."[35]

Questions for Reflection

1. Does your church suffer from a "generation gap"?
2. Is the level of intergenerational conflict in your church more or less frequent than what occurs in the broader culture? Why do you think this is the case?
3. What is your greatest difficulty when it comes to relating to leaders older than you? What about when relating to those younger than you?
4. What values do you feel are most important to maintain when navigating a church conflict based on intergenerational differences?
5. How can thinking about leadership succession and a congregation's long-term health help a church overcome intergenerational suspicion?
6. How might the three deferential virtues of showing preference for others, intentional self-denial, and gracious withdrawal help churches overcome intergenerational tensions? What would this look like in your church?

9

LIVING LIKE OUTSIDERS

The war against Japan had been over for nearly thirty years when Hiroo Onada walked out of the Philippine jungle and "surrendered." The war was over, the world had changed, and Onada returned to Japan—as a man from an earlier time and an alien in his native land. "There are so many tall buildings and automobiles in Tokyo," he lamented.

The church has reason to feel similarly. It is adrift in a world that does not share its values or recognize its authority. According to Rod Dreher, author of *The Benedict Option*, the culture war is over, and biblical conservatives have lost. "The culture war that began with the sexual revolution in the 1960s has now ended in defeat for Christian conservatives," Dreher states.[1] "The cultural left—which is to say, the American mainstream—has no intention of living in postwar peace. It is pressing forward with a harsh, relentless occupation, one that is aided by the cluelessness of Christians who don't understand what's happening."[2]

Dreher's proposed solution, however, is not to retreat into the jungle and fight on but to put down roots. His counsel feels a bit like the instruction given to the Babylonian exiles in Jeremiah 29:4–7:

> This is what the LORD Almighty, the God of Israel, says to all those I carried into exile from Jerusalem to Babylon: "Build houses and settle down; plant gardens and eat what they produce. Marry and have sons and daughters; find wives for your sons and give your daughters in marriage, so that they too may have sons and daughters. Increase in number there; do not decrease. Also, seek the peace and prosperity of the city to which I have carried you into exile. Pray to the LORD for it, because if it prospers, you too will prosper."

God was doing more than telling His people to make the best of a bad situation. False prophets had peddled a different vision of the future to God's people. First, they had assured them that the exile would never happen. God would not judge His people and drive them from their homeland. When judgment came, the false prophets predicted that the exile would be short—only a year, maybe two at the most (Jer. 29:27–28). But Jeremiah's message indicated otherwise. God's people weren't going home anytime soon. They were going to be gone long enough to plant and harvest, long enough to have children and watch them grow. Indeed, their exile would last long enough to see their children marry and have children of their own. This exile would last years, decades even. Indeed, those who did the math in Jeremiah 29:10 surely must have recognized that for many of them, it would last the rest of their lives.

This is what it means to be an exile. It is the status of those the Bible calls aliens or strangers. An older word for it is *sojourner*. A sojourner is someone who is from somewhere else—a temporary resident in a place that he does not think of as home. It is the word Abraham used to describe himself as he lived like a foreigner in the land that God had promised to give him (Gen. 23:4; see also Heb. 11:9). It is also the word that the Bible uses to describe the church (see 1 Peter 2:11 ESV). To be a sojourner is to be a permanent outsider.

THE ART OF BEING A SOJOURNER

It's not easy being an outsider. People look at you funny, because you stand out from the crowd. They don't speak the same language or eat the same food that you do. They don't play by the same rules. Outsider status is part of the church's calling. In 2 Corinthians 6:14–16, the apostle Paul urges,

> Do not be yoked together with unbelievers. For what do righteousness and wickedness have in common? Or what fellowship can light have with darkness? What harmony is there between Christ and Belial? Or what does a believer have in common with an unbeliever? What agreement is there between the temple of God and idols? For we are the temple of the living God. As God has said: "I will live with them and walk among them, and I will be their God, and they will be my people."

Paul's prescription in verse 17 to "come out" and "be separate" sounds old-fashioned. It seems more like the outmoded philosophy of an era when the rules of Christian living were "Don't drink, don't chew, and don't go out with them that do." It must certainly sound odd to a church culture whose worship services are mostly concerned with making people feel comfortable. We would rather show others how much we have in common with them than emphasize our differences.

But Paul's admonition was addressed to a church that had fallen too much in step with the values and practices of the culture that surrounded it. The Corinthian church had trouble breaking with its religious and cultural past. The lingering scent from old altars still enticed them into idolatry and sexual immorality. They had trouble finding a cohesive center for their own community life. The Corinthian believers were as self-centered and individualistic in their internal allegiances as they were in their worship and ministry (see 1 Cor. 1:12; 3:4; 11:17–22; 14:26). They were lacking the two basic characteristics essential for successful sojourning: a strong sense of being different from the surrounding culture and an equally strong sense of being the same as other Christians.

A sojourner is someone whose roots and customs come from somewhere else. This is the kind of difference that prompts others to say, "You're not from around here, are you?" But the secret to Christian sojourning is to be different about the right things. The five contrasts that Paul describes in 2 Corinthians 6:14–16 relate to of lifestyle, understanding, identification, faith, and calling.

FIVE IMPORTANT DIFFERENCES

Christian sojourners are marked by their righteousness. Righteousness is a gift that comes to us by grace through our faith in the saving work of Jesus Christ. It is also a practice. However, there is more to the art of Christian practice than a short list of approved or disapproved behaviors. A list is sometimes important, but it is not enough. Righteousness is a dynamic or a *lifestyle* that is introduced into our lives by the Holy Spirit. It is the concrete expression of the new life that comes to us through Jesus Christ. This is not a form of spiritual perfectionism. If righteous behavior were automatic for us, the apostle would not have needed to provide a list of contrasts between the characteristics of a believer and an unbeliever.

The righteous practice that marks the Christian life also does not come to us fully formed in an instant. It is not like the gift of our righteous position in Christ that we receive all at once. One important implication of this is that we may find those who are truly Christians at various stages in their development. We may also find inconsistencies, which is precisely why Paul felt it was necessary to underscore these contrasts in 2 Corinthians 6:14–16. "Christian Miss Bates may have an unkinder tongue than unbelieving Dick Firkin," C. S. Lewis points out. "That, by itself, does not tell us whether Christianity works. The question is what Miss Bates's tongue would be like if she were not a Christian and what Dick's would be like if he became one."[3] We might describe this as a growing habit of righteousness. Many of our patterns of thinking and behavior have been ingrained in us from birth and are shaped by the learned assumptions of a variety of influences in our culture.

Because those who follow Christ are sojourners in their own native culture, they must often unlearn as much as they learn.

In order for both kinds of learning to take place, there has to be *knowledge*. We need to know the things that the Bible regards as righteous and those things it considers to be unrighteous. The assumptions we have held all our lives must be tested by a measure other than the standards of our own conviction or those of our culture. This is why a lifestyle that can properly be called Christian grows out of understanding. Paul underscores this necessity when he contrasts light with darkness. To be a Christian sojourner is to be enlightened. This does not mean that those who follow Christ are smarter than everyone else. And it does not imply that Christians are naturally better than anyone else. It means that they now see things in a way that they did not previously. Paul says something even stronger in Ephesians 5:8: "For you were once darkness, but now you are light in the Lord. Live as children of light." Not only do we see things differently than we did before, but we ourselves are different. It isn't only the fact that we have "seen the light" that has led to such a change, but something far more fundamental has happened. We *have become* light.

The contrast highlighting this in 2 Corinthians 6:15 is between Christ and Belial. The title Belial is probably derived from a Hebrew word meaning "worthless." It was used to refer to Satan by the Qumran community and spoke of Satan as the one who opposes God. Elsewhere, the apostle Paul says that prior to our union with Christ, we were in alliance with Satan. We followed the ways of this world and Satan himself (Eph. 2:2). This does not mean, however, that we were devil worshipers. Paul uses the language of citizenship. The way that we lived was a combined function of cultural learning and unthinking allegiance. All of this changed when we were made alive with Christ. The interjection of God's grace into our experience radically changed our status in this old domain from insider to outsider. We are now "from" somewhere else and under new authority (Eph. 2:5–6). We no longer identify with our old identity. We see ourselves as citizens of a different kingdom, whose values are incompatible with those of our former master.

A change of citizenship paves the way to a new *identity*. Someone who takes the oath receives the right to call themselves a citizen of the United States. Those whose allegiance is transferred from Satan to Christ receive the right to designate themselves as "believers." This means that Christian sojourning begins with an act of faith. The label "Christian" is not merely a cultural designation but also a relational one. A Christian is someone who has put their faith in the person and work of Jesus Christ. A Christian is also someone who has embraced "the faith"—that body of truths handed down to the church by Christ and the apostles. This means that the title "believer" binds those who take it upon themselves to the word of God. If Christian sojourning is partly a matter of being different about the right things, how do we know what the right things are? They cannot be a matter of personal taste. The label of *believer* is a reminder that the lifestyle of those who identify with Jesus is shaped by the revealed truth of God's Word. The Word that informs our understanding also tests our assumptions. However, the title of *believer* also implies something critical about our relationship to the Word. It indicates that we have responded to it. It is not enough to simply know the Bible or even hold the Bible in high regard. There are many who would not consider themselves Christian who consider the Bible valuable. To say that I am a believer implies that I have staked my life on it. I will allow what God has said in His Word to define me and set the pattern for my life.

All of this unfolds within the larger framework of the *life calling* that the Bible describes as worship. The contrast underscoring this in 2 Corinthians 6:16 is between the temple of God and idols. We are the temple of God. Paul's use of the collective "we" in v. 16 is important because it helps us understand the context of this statement. He is not just talking about the individual believer. It is certainly true that the believer's body is a temple of the Holy Spirit (1 Cor. 6:19). But the context of 2 Corinthians 6:16 is a larger one. Here, Paul is speaking of the church. This places the Christian's sojourning experience within a larger framework than one of personal values and individual practice. Christian sojourning is a community experience. We were not meant to sojourn alone.

Paul's designation of the church as a temple is important for another reason. If Christian sojourning is itself a mode of worship, then it expands our frame of reference beyond thinking of ourselves simply as a community that we call the church. If Christian living were only a matter of following through on the values and practices of those who call themselves Christian, we would only be adding one more tribe to the vast multitude that already exist. In a horizontal frame of reference that takes only human difference into account, there is really nothing to set the Christian's lifestyle apart from anyone else's. The Christian's differences may seem more attractive when they are compared to the values and practices of others, but there is nothing about the Christian's practices that would necessarily make them obligatory. If my only frame of reference is a human one, everybody has the right to choose the lifestyle they prefer. You may select a lifestyle that I consider degraded, but that is really just my opinion. Once God is introduced into the mix, though, everything changes. To speak of the church as the temple of God places God at the center of who we are and what we do. Christians not only have different values and practices from the domain that Paul refers to as the "world" but are under an entirely different jurisdiction.

The difference between Christian sojourners and everyone else is more than merely taste or preference. It is a matter of recognizing God's rightful place in the world as its Creator and Supreme Ruler. When this vertical dimension of God is added to the picture, Christian lifestyle becomes a matter of obedience. This obedience is, in turn, a mode of worship. Contemporary believers are used to thinking of worship as an event. Even more narrowly, we often think of worship primarily as the musical portion of the church service. But the command of Romans 12:1 that those belonging to Christ are to offer their bodies as living sacrifices reveals the Bible's picture of what constitutes worship—and it is far more expansive than contemporary thinking on the matter. Music is certainly an aspect of Christian worship, as is the church's "worship" service. But the church's worship service is really only one dimension of biblical worship. Worship is also what I do everywhere else. The person I am on the job, in the home, or at a baseball game with my friends are all expressions of the kind of worship that Paul describes in Romans 12:1. In other words, worship is not a single act but an entire lifestyle.

At the same time, the Bible's vision of a lifestyle of worship does not marginalize the place of congregational worship in the life of the believer. If anything, it elevates its importance. This is because, by Paul's definition, we are always part of some kind of collective worship. James K. A. Smith writes of the undermining effect of what he calls the "secular liturgies" of culture on the thinking and practice of Christians. Secular liturgies are repeated practices that are value-laden and have behind them a vision of the world as it ought to be but is at odds with God's vision. These liturgies do not always occur in contexts we would consider to be religious in the technical sense. In fact, most of the time they do not. But by Smith's definition, they are religious in the sense that "they are institutions that command our allegiance, that vie for our passion, and that aim to capture our heart with a particular vision of the good life. They don't want to just give us entertainment and education; they want to make us into certain kinds of people."[4]

This larger definition of what constitutes a liturgy might be expressed by school, a political party, the latest blockbuster from Marvel, or the primary example that Smith uses: the shopping mall. All of these cultural institutions perform functions that approximate worship. They include rituals of ultimate concern that form our identity, because they reflect and shape what matters most to us.[5] Smith notes that instead of undermining these secular liturgies with its own teaching, practices, and especially its worship, the church does the opposite. This is especially true of the culture's "liturgies of consumerism." Smith writes, "Rather than properly countering the liturgy of consumption, the church ends up mimicking it, merely substituting Christian commodities—'Jesusfied' versions of worldly products, which are acquired, accumulated, and disposed of to make room for the new and the novel."[6] How do we counter this? What must we do in order to show the right kind of difference that will set us apart as Christian sojourners? The answer is that we need to cultivate the right kind of similarities.

THE IMPORTANCE OF BEING THE SAME

American culture loves a rebel. From Charlie Chaplin's tramp to Harrison Ford's Han Solo, one of the enduring themes in pop culture is that of the lovable misfit. This is the person who doesn't fit in. He or she stands apart from the crowd and often views it with contempt. It is a vision grounded in a philosophy of rugged individualism. This person doesn't need anybody else to get by.

It's not that we are unfamiliar with or even opposed to a group experience. But even in our groups, we tend to view ourselves through the lens of individualism. This individualistic note is often combined with the consumerism described above by Smith. This affects our sense of belonging to the church. Many of us belong to our church the way we belong to a fitness club. Our belonging is linked to our sense that we are getting some benefit from it. If that changes, we have no problem "belonging" to a different church. Some of us may even think of ourselves as belonging to several churches, each one providing a different benefit. We like one because of the preaching, another because of the music, and perhaps even a third because of its architecture or setting.

There is certainly nothing wrong with expecting to benefit from the local church and its ministries. But a consumerist mindset can make it difficult for us to establish relationships.

"It is not hard to conclude that the major single problem for American social life is the problem of relationships—we do not understand them and cannot maintain them," William Dyrness observes. "We have seen that one of the historical roots for this problem is the tendency to define ourselves in economic or material terms. We find our meaning more often in our possessions, and the status they confer, than in our relationships."[7]

The experience of the New Testament church was radically different. According to Acts 2:44–47,

> All the believers were together and had everything in common. They sold property and possessions to give to anyone who had need. Every day they continued to meet together in the temple courts. They broke bread in their homes and ate together with glad and sincere hearts, praising God and enjoying the favor of all the people. And the Lord added to their number daily those who were being saved.

The lifestyle that Luke describes here has been viewed by some as an economic experiment that was later abandoned. But the description of the early church's treatment of their possessions is merely a concrete illustration of the church's sense of solidarity. According to New Testament scholar F. F. Bruce, the Greek phrase translated "together" (v. 44) conveys the same idea that Paul expresses in different language in 1 Corinthians 11:18 when he speaks of God's people coming together "as a church."[8] What today's consumeristic individualism robs us of is this experience of being "all together."

Cultivating a sense of *all-togetherness* is just as necessary to the art of Christian sojourning as having an awareness of how we differ from the rest of society. It is doubtful that we can sustain a pattern of life as outsiders for very long without finding some context where we can feel like insiders. Highly individualistic cultures like our own are still sensitive to rejection by the group. Even those who see themselves as cultural outsiders will find affinity groups that share their sense of alienation. Parents often worry about how negative peer pressure affects their adolescent children. Yet the truth is that every age and every group is subject to this kind of pressure. Missiologist Donald K. Smith notes, "The fear of rejection haunts most people. Rejection from the group is a severe sanction, to be avoided at almost any cost. Acceptance by a group can be such a pleasurable, even necessary, thing that an individual will voluntarily change behavior to conform to group patterns."[9] It's not by chance that the most extreme penalty the church can mete out when it disciplines offenders is expulsion from the congregation (see Matt. 18:17; 1 Cor. 5:1–11).

FIVE MARKS OF BELONGING

Along with the five characteristics that contrast the Christian sojourner from the world in 2 Corinthians 6:14–16, Paul also includes five marks of belonging. These are partnership, fellowship, harmony, commonality, and agreement. If the contrasts in these verses provide the polarity that enables us to maintain a healthy distance from those aspects of our culture that are incompatible with our Christian identity, these five marks create the nucleus around which our alternative identity should be formed.

The first element included in Paul's list is *partnership*.

This is expressed both in the metaphor of the yoke and by the Greek word in v. 16 that the NIV translates with the phrase "in common." It conveys the idea of sharing or participating in something. It is well suited to the imagery of the yoke, which points to the church's vocational identity. The members of the church are bound together in a common task. In the context of Paul's rebuke to the Corinthians, this language reproves them for their tendency to align themselves with teachers who do not act in the best interests of the church.

Preaching and teaching equip the church to accomplish its calling. According to Ephesians 4:11–13, those who minister the Word prepare the church to fulfill its ministry. But by yoking themselves to the wrong kind of teachers, the Corinthians were sharing the church's task with those whose agenda was incompatible with its mission (2 Cor. 11:13). Worship of their favorite speakers undermined their sense of shared vocation. Church members acted as if the status of their favorite teacher somehow accrued to them. The result was a hypercompetitive culture divided along party lines (1 Cor. 1:11–12). Paul's reproof reminded them that by aligning themselves first with Christ, they were also aligned with one another. Christ is not divided.

This does not mean, however, that we lose our individuality when we come to Christ. Individualism is not the same as individuality. Our nature as individuals does not suddenly disappear when we are united to Christ. We are not absorbed into a group mind. To the contrary, individuality is actually part of God's design for the church. It is just as damaging to the church when we refuse to recognize the distinctiveness of each member as it is for an individual member to reject the whole. Our different backgrounds, personalities, and gifts are engrafted into the body of Christ by the working of the Holy Spirit: "Just as a body, though one, has many parts, but all its many parts form one body, so it is with Christ" (1 Cor. 12:12).

The second mark of belonging that Paul lists in 2 Corinthians 6:14–16 is *fellowship*. When most of us speak of having fellowship in church, we are usually referring to the small talk that takes place after the service. There is nothing wrong with conversation over coffee and donuts, but it isn't necessarily fellowship. Fellowship is not the same as socializing, though it may have a social dimension to it. Biblical fellowship involves the mutual sharing of identity and experience. To experience fellowship is to continue together. More than simply being in the same space, it is a sustained and determined sense of belonging together.

In dichotomizing light and darkness in v. 14, Paul links fellowship to a shared experience of enlightenment. This is also a shared identity. Not only are Christian sojourners those who have seen the light, they *are* light (Eph. 5:8), as was iterated earlier. This speaks of a shared nature as well as a common experience of transformation: "For you were once darkness, but now you are light in the Lord. Live as children of light" (Eph. 5:8). What we are now is not what we once were. Baptism is the community rite that signals this change. Its imagery of washing combined with burial and resurrection provides a tangible reminder of what has happened to us in Christ. Its observance *in the congregation* serves as a regular reminder of our new identity while at the same time pointing us to the obligation we have to live a different kind of life (Rom. 6:4; Col. 2:11–12).

New life brings with it a different sensibility. When we are joined to Jesus Christ we are introduced to a whole new order of existence. The term that the New Testament uses to speak of this is *kingdom* (Luke 17:20–21; Acts 8:12; 14:22; Rom. 14:17; 1 Cor. 4:20). The kingdom is the realm of God's power and Christ's dominion. One day, it will be made concrete when Jesus returns and is enthroned in Jerusalem. But for now, we experience its reality within us as the Holy Spirit enables us to acknowledge Christ's rule over our own lives. One of the Holy Spirit's most important ministries in this is to give us the mind of Christ about this new order.

The word Paul uses to describe this agreement in 2 Corinthians 6:15 is translated *harmony*, our third mark of belonging. This word has its roots in the musical realm. It is the Greek term from which we get the word *symphony*. But in the New Testament era, it was mainly used in contexts that dealt with relationships. In 2 Corinthians 6:15, Paul employs it to express the discord between Christ and Satan. They are not on the same page. In doing so, Paul was also exposing something about the Corinthian church. His assumption was that those who are in Christ will side with Christ. And if they side with Christ, then they should side with one another.

Christian sojourners are not always the same as one another, to be sure. We don't look the same. We don't always like the same style of preaching or music. We don't all worship in the same way. Some of us are outgoing, and others are shy. We may even disagree profoundly over politics. But we all share one overarching universal trait. We all agree with Christ. We do not always agree with one another about what we think Christ meant. But as far as we're able to understand what He said, we agree with Him.

Or to be more accurate, we agree that we ought to agree

with Christ. Again, it is important to bear in mind that Paul's warning to the Corinthians suggests that some in this church had fallen out of step with gospel teaching. They did not mean to side with Satan, the great adversary of Christ and the church. Indeed, it is highly unlikely that they thought of themselves as being on Satan's side. Paul's reproof evinces that they had inadvertently aligned themselves with God's enemy.

The fourth mark of belonging that defines the church's sojourning experience is *commonality*. The Greek word translated as "common" in v. 15 refers to a "portion" or "share." Sometimes I come across other believers whose cultural background lifestyle, and personal interests are so far from my own that I cannot imagine how we might carry on a conversation. Yet I have more in common with them than I do with an unbeliever who shares every aspect of my personality and background. The differences existing between those who believe and those who do not are irreconcilable. Believers and unbelievers face two radically different futures and hold fundamentally different assumptions.

While Paul recognized the fundamental differences between those in Christ and those outside of Him, he sought to capitalize on the commonality he *did* have with outsiders. This is seen when he described himself as the apostle to the gentiles (Rom. 11:13; Gal. 2:8). He based his missionary efforts on a strategy of similarity. As much as he was able, Paul became like those he sought to reach. In order for this to be true, there had to be some points of common ground between him and those to whom he ministered.

While believers and unbelievers have many differences, they still have much in common. They both were created by

God. They share a common experience of sin. They may have similar cultural backgrounds and aspirations when it comes to the common details of life. They want health and happiness. They want good for their children.

Still, the experience of God's grace in Christ places those that the Bible calls *believers* in a category of their own. Believers have benefits that the unbeliever does not have. Chief among them are the hope of heaven and the right to address God as Father.

In our effort to create a point of contact with unbelievers we sometimes minimize these differences. We may say something like, "I am just like you." But this is not actually true. It would be more accurate to say, "I was once like you." The work of Christ introduces a great divide that separates the believer from the unbeliever. Our sins are forgiven. Our nature has been changed. We have a destiny that the unbeliever does not. The portion or share that comes to those who are in Jesus Christ belongs to them alone. This is no ground for arrogance. If anything, the recognition of these differences should humble us and motivate us to invite unbelievers to transfer their allegiance and join the ranks of those who believe. The difference that Paul describes by this dichotomy in 2 Corinthians 6:15 does not imply a posture of aloofness toward the unbelieving world. Quite the opposite: "I am obligated both to Greeks and non-Greeks, both to the wise and the foolish" (Rom. 1:14).

The fifth mark of our all-togetherness is *agreement*. Paul mentions it in 2 Corinthians 6:16 when he points to the discord between the temple of God and idols. This is the sort of agreement you find when a group reaches a consensus. Everybody is on the same page. It is the kind of unity we experience when the vote is called and the result is unanimous. The contrast that

Paul paints in this verse mirrors one expressed in 1 Corinthians 10:21: "You cannot drink the cup of the Lord and the cup of demons too; you cannot have a part in both the Lord's table and the table of demons." Some in the Corinthian church continued to participate in idol feasts, perhaps for pragmatic reasons. They rationalized their presence by saying that the idol did not exist (1 Cor. 8:4). This was technically true but theologically incomplete. The fact that the idol did not exist did not automatically mean that there was no spiritual activity taking place when the idol was worshiped. There was a kind of spiritual fellowship taking place—not with the idol, but with the demons who inspired such worship (1 Cor. 10:19–20).

Paul's main point in 2 Corinthians 6:16 is really about identity. His reasoning seems like a variation on a common axiom employed in architecture: "Form follows function." Only in this case, Paul is saying, "Function reflects form." The idol has no place in the temple of God because it is the temple of *God*. The believer has no place at the table of demons because they partake of the cup of the Lord. It is Paul's way of saying, "Remember who you are!" Like the Israelites living in Babylon, we too are exiles in a land not our home. It might be the factory or school where we work. It could be the neighborhood in which we live. For some, it might even be the family to which we were born. Although we once may have felt like we belonged in these contexts, a growing awareness of our Christian identity has left us feeling like misfits. Our Christianity may also have introduced an element of tension into relationships that once felt comfortable to us. Those who used to regard us as friends and family now treat us like strangers.

It's no wonder, then, that we sometimes find ourselves

hunkered down in a defensive posture, only dashing out of our jungle compound in brief forays to replenish our supplies. On those few occasions when we attempt to brave the culture in hopes that we can make inroads for the gospel, the landscape we find seems so radically changed. This is not the world as we remember it. Should we be surprised? Jesus warned His disciples, "Do not suppose that I have come to bring peace to the earth. I did not come to bring peace, but a sword. For I have come to turn 'a man against his father, a daughter against her mother, a daughter-in-law against her mother-in-law—a man's enemies will be the members of his own household'" (Matt. 10:34–36).

Christian sojourners have a spiritual identity that sets them apart from non-Christians. It inevitably makes us outsiders. Yet our identity as sojourners also provides us with a context for belonging. We are members of a community spanning earth and heaven. Although we come from every tribe and tongue, we speak the same vocabulary of faith and share a common experience of grace. We possess a wide variety of spiritual gifts and God-given abilities, but are engaged in the same mission. We can also lay claim to the same promise, the promise of home. This promise is grounded in the certainty of God's presence and the assurance that we are His people: "As God has said: 'I will live with them and walk among them, and I will be their God, and they will be my people'" (2 Cor. 6:16). This is a promise that we experience even now.

Even if culture wars ended, the church's sojourn has not. We continue to be pilgrims. Like Abraham, we are called to live as strangers in a foreign country. Like him, we are also looking for a city whose architect and builder is God: "For here we do not have an enduring city, but we are looking for the city that is to come" (Heb. 13:14). The glorious vision of New Jerusalem is a picture of that city (Rev. 21:2–4). It's true that it doesn't look like any city we have ever visited. Nor does the atmosphere described in Revelation sound like any church we have ever attended. But that is because John is giving us a vision of the church's future. This is the church at the end of its pilgrimage. It is the church as it will be after it has returned from exile. For now, we must be the people of God wherever we find ourselves. Settle in. Put down roots. Welcome home, at least for now.

Questions for Reflection

1. Are you comfortable with your identity as a sojourner, or is it one you resist? Why?

2. What does it look like to be a Christian sojourner in your local setting?

3. Think of a conflict in your church or small-group setting. How might cultivating one of the five marks of belonging (partnership, fellowship, harmony, commonality, and agreement) offer a path toward resolution?

4. What are some practical steps you might take to cultivate the marks of belonging? What obstacles do you face?

5. How will recognizing that believers are different from the world yet similar to one another foster and maintain unity in local churches?

10

FINAL THOUGHTS

So what have we learned about ourselves, our identity, and our differences? Thinking about these issues can be dizzying. They all seem so nebulous. At times, they may seem too abstract to act upon. Thinking about the way we *think* is hard work. It's like watching a 3D movie without 3D glasses. After a while, everything is a blur. It may be helpful to distill everything covered thus far into nine important principles for being all together different.

NINE PRINCIPLES
FOR MOVING FORWARD

Principle #1: Embrace the blessed mess of being different. Perhaps one of the reasons we struggle so much in accepting and navigating our differences is because they complicate our lives. We have a difficult time understanding ourselves, let alone those who are not like us. We don't enjoy the conflict that our differences engender. Because we long for simplicity and order, we tend to be overly simplistic and romanticize our notions of congregational diversity. So here is the fundamental starting point:

Different is good. Our foundational differences have their origin in God's design. Difference is also complementary. In a way, our God-given differences reflect a divinely designed mutual weakness that should force us to recognize how dependent we are upon one another—and ultimately upon God.

But it is just as important to embrace the problems that our differences create. Not that our differences per se create problems: our sin creates them. To embrace does not mean to enjoy or even to capitulate to them. It simply means that with God's grace, we will face them head on. We do not need to be afraid of our differences, but we do need to acknowledge how the collateral damage of sin has affected them. Being different is good, but it is also difficult. Only the grace and truth of God can enable us to be all together and different at the same time.

Principle #2: Allow faith to transform your identity. By faith, we mean more than affirming a set of truths. Cognitive affirmation of God's truth is certainly necessary for faith, but faith is also a matter of commitment. Faith begins with a commitment to God, and it reflects a confidence in His ordering of our lives.

We are who we are because He is the God of our history. If the number of hairs on our head have been determined by God (Matt. 10:30; Luke 12:7), so have our other features. The color of our skin, our physical abilities and limitations, and our DNA are all part of God's plan for our lives. Our personal narrative orients us to who we are, and God is the ultimate author of that narrative. The people we live among have shaped both who and what we are committed to, but we are also part of a much larger community of faith that spans both heaven and earth. This larger community (the body of Christ) does not blot out our earthly ties, but it does take precedence over them. It also provides us with different commitments and boundaries that take priority over all others. This means that our identity is not fixed but is continually being formed by Christ. This is a long-term project that will be completed in the bodily resurrection. Understanding ourselves and those around us is a discipline of faith grounded in hope and expressed in love.

Principle #3: Only God can tell you who you really are. There are too many forces in play that tell us to trust our own judgment and that we are to determine our own identity. If we are to discover our true identity, we must find it by looking in the mirror of God's Word. Careful examination will show that we are royal children created in God's image and have been called and empowered by Him to act as His stewards in the world He created. Although the divine image has been marred by sin, God's grace has given us a new identity that is being renewed according to the image of Christ. Because of this, we don't need to succumb to the temptation of false perfectionism. We can be honest about our shortcomings and failures without giving in to them. Changed behavior begins with changed perceptions. We must see ourselves differently if we are to live differently. But this change in the way we view ourselves does not come without a measure of intentionality. Transformation begins with identity. We are as we come to see ourselves. We come to see ourselves differently by training our attention upon the truth of God's Word and ultimately, upon Christ Himself.

Principle #4: We are us, and they are them. When God said it was not good for humanity to be alone, He wasn't just talking about marriage. There is an important corporate dimension to our identity. Group identity is shaped by comparing myself to those who are part of the group to which I belong. This is an act of inclusion and exclusion. While I see myself as an insider, as far as the group is concerned, I view those not part of it as outsiders. The same dynamic that makes the church feel close to those who are on the inside will make it feel closed to those who are not.

In reality, churches are a collection of many groups. If they are to be effective, they must have an overarching identity that trumps all others. This can only happen through transformative communication guided by Scripture and the Spirit, who enables believers to develop an awareness of their in-Christ social identity. We are not members of only one group. We are part of many groups and, in a sense, possess multiple identities. These identities are nested like Russian dolls, with one functioning as an overarching or superordinate identity. For the believer, this superordinate identity is the one we share with all other believers. This overarching identity as a Christian does not wipe out our other identities. Instead, it reorients them. Intergroup tension is a major source of conflict in the life of the church and must be dealt with by learning to relate to one another based on our primary identity. This can happen only if we learn about and embrace those whom we have learned to see as the "other."

Principle #5: It's not all about me. It's about us. The Bible helps us understand that our identity is individual and collective. We do not lose our sense of self when we become part of the body of Christ. But the nature of life in the church sometimes requires that we subordinate those things that give us our sense of individuality to our collective identity in Christ.

It's not wrong to embrace one's national, ethnic, or political identity. Yet for the one who belongs to Christ, none of these can be primary. Recognizing our collective identity in Christ has practical implications. It means that each of us must have a regard for the other. It helps those who are in the church to stop relating to one another in an "us" versus "them" way. The church is not a Borg Collective. Both individual and communal identities have roles to play in our experience. Our task as followers of Christ is to master our multiple identities and learn how our individual distinctiveness contributes to the whole.

Principle #6: Race and ethnicity still matter. Concerns about race and ethnicity did not fade into the background after the Civil Rights Act of 1964. If anything, these issues are more in the forefront of our thinking than ever before. Race and ethnicity still matter, but should they?

Racial and ethnic differences continue to be relevant in Christ. Social categories like Jew, Greek, slave, or free are realigned within the context of our baptismal identity. We do not need to suppress these social categories. Nor do we have to be ashamed of them. We do, however, have to see them within a hierarchy that places our master identity, as one who is in Christ, first. Whatever else we are, we are in Christ first and foremost. This master identity aligns us with everyone else who is in Christ. Being in Christ does not bring about a "raceless race," and the work of racial and ethnic reconciliation must be sought within the context of these identities instead of to the exclusion of them.

Principle #7: Sex is more than having sex, and identity is more than a decision. The biblical idea of sex involves more than having sex. Today's culture says that I am who I am based on sexual attraction or personal choice. The Bible, on the other hand, grounds human identity in an identity that is God given and that begins with the biological differentiation of male or female.

One of the first things we learn about human identity in Scripture is that it has a sexual dimension. God created humans to be male and female. This male/female design has implications beyond biological function. It reflects a relational interdependence that ultimately points us to our need for God. The importance of being male and female is not limited to the biology of reproduction or the experience of sexual intimacy. It is a foundational difference that shapes relationships in the home and in the church.

The church's response to our culture's shifting ideas about sexual practice and identity has tended toward a culture-war approach, which typically states the *what* of human sexuality but not the *how*. It has little to offer those who struggle with their sexual practice and identity. An alternative to the culture-war approach is one that is relational. This is an approach that begins with the person instead of the position, with relationship rather than rebuke. It begins with the simple step of inviting someone into your life and community.

Principle #8: One generation goes, and another comes— but not without struggle. Growing older is tough to accept. Being young is equally difficult. Different generations bring with them different values. The challenge of generational identity is not just the way we see ourselves but the way we see others. Generational differences can provide a healthy balance of perspectives in the church, but they are just as liable to lead to crossed signals. The presence of as many as five different generations is creating fault lines in the relational landscape of congregational life. Ethnically homogenous churches face added challenges. Congregations whose culture has been shaped by first-generation immigrants must also cope with the challenge of a second generation that is drawn to a style of church with a more Americanized culture. They often have difficulty holding on to second-generation youth. Ethnic churches also deal with issues of poverty and alienation. Overall, the American church is having trouble transferring power from one generation to another.

Despite these difficulties, the church's generational differences have the potential to create a community whose strengths complement one another. The secret to creating a multigenerational community that values one another begins with the recognition that our mutual strengths are also our greatest weaknesses. We must also acknowledge that multigenerational community comes with a measure of shared discomfort. We will not immediately appreciate the gifts that others bring to the community. The key to successful community demands that we become practiced in the deferential virtues: showing preference for others, intentional self-denial, and gracious withdrawal.

Principle #9: Don't be afraid to live like an outsider. One of the overarching identities that Scripture assigns to those who follow Christ is that of an outsider or sojourner. It's not an easy or comfortable status to have. A sojourner is someone whose roots and customs come from somewhere else. The goal is not simply to be different but to be different about the right things.

In 2 Corinthians 6:14–16, we find five contrasts that show us how to be different in the right way. Christian sojourners live a different lifestyle. They do the right things. This is not spiritual perfectionism but a progressive growth in holiness, which demands that they unlearn sinful habits just as much as they learn holy habits. Christian sojourners also have a different understanding. They know what the Bible regards as righteous. They have a new identity. They are "believers." This new name binds Christ followers to the Word of God. It is a reminder that their lifestyle must be shaped by the revealed truth of God's Word. All of this unfolds within the larger framework of the life calling of worship. Worship is more than an event for the Christian. It is a lifestyle.

Along with the five contrasts characteristic of Christian sojourners in 2 Corinthians 6:14–16, Paul also includes five marks of belonging. Partnership, fellowship, harmony, commonality, and agreement create the nucleus around which the believer's alternative identity should be formed.

FOUR NOT-SO-SIMPLE STEPS

Knowing the principles is a start, but it is only a start. Perhaps the more pressing question for us is what we should do with what we know? Andy Crouch rightly notes, "We don't make Culture, we make omelets. We tell stories. We build hospitals. We pass laws."[1] It is not enough to simply *think* about culture. We want to *shape* culture. Jesus told His disciples, "Now that you know these things, you will be blessed if you do them" (John 13:17). But what does it mean to *do* identity? If Andy Crouch is right about culture, then we can't make this particular omelet without cracking some eggs. This will mean, first of all, taking steps to become comfortable with our own discomfort.

Socrates observed that the unexamined life is not worth

living. When it comes to identity, it is not possible to live an unexamined life. We begin by giving ourselves permission to explore our differences and the reasons for the discomfort we feel about them. This must be a communal exercise if it is to make a difference.

One of the greatest obstacles we face when it comes to affirming our unity while honoring our uniqueness is our penchant for denial and one-sided conversation. Dealing with the mutual discomfort that our differences create seems simple enough; we just admit to one another that we have a problem. It rarely works that way. In the beginning, the conversation is almost always one-sided. Our discussions are often tinged with anger. Unless at least one of the parties in the conversation responds with grace and patience, things are not liable to end well.

Some years ago I (John) had a disagreement with a colleague whose cultural background differed from mine. The disagreement was largely due to my inability (or unwillingness) to see the issue through his cultural lens. During our discussion, my responses became increasingly heated, until at last I crossed the line from appropriate argumentation to rudeness. The next day, I was surprised to receive a message from him asking if we could meet. I agreed, but with a certain amount of fear. He was a vice-president in our organization, and I knew I had behaved badly. Instead of taking me to task, he welcomed me with a smile. "I wanted to talk to you," he said, "because I know you are a good thinker and what you had to say was important to you. I want to be sure that I understand." We had a long discussion about the matter. When I left, I understood his position much better. What is more, I felt affirmed. To this day, I remain deeply moved by his humility, patience, and grace toward me. The fact that he listened to me taught me the importance of listening to him. I don't think it would have happened if he had not made the first move in my direction.

We cannot have this kind of conversation without a forum. For this reason, the second step is to provide a community "table" where we can come together to listen and communicate (in that order). As you might expect, this is harder than it sounds. A community table is more than a meeting. It is a safe space where people can learn to trust one another and speak frankly to one another. It is a place where we make a commitment to help one another to be the best version of ourselves. This means that we will make a commitment to patience and accountability. Patience means that we will bear with one another's failures and blind spots. The path to mutual understanding is a long one. Accountability means that we will commit ourselves to helping one another when we cross the line. This means we will call one another back to civility when the conversation veers toward incivility. We will expect emotion to be expressed but we will remind one another to express it with care.

In the beginning at least, the table probably needs to be small. Small groups will serve better than large congregational meetings for this. The church will need to equip and empower those who have been gifted by God to moderate group conversation and mediate disputes. This will certainly require practice. It may also demand training. The church's leadership team is probably a good starting place. Once they have learned the art of leading a group in awkward conversations, they can model it for others.

The third step is to acquire a new vocabulary and conceptual framework for understanding what divides us. We need to learn to think about the way we think. At the present, our discussions about identity and difference are largely polemic, rife with clichés and slogans. We talk about identity, dignity, and justice without asking what these terms actually mean. Biblical teaching and group exploration will help the church see itself and its interpersonal conflicts as identity problems rather than ethical problems or personality flaws.

The fourth step is to take a chance. Risk opening the door of your life to those not like you. This doesn't need to be a radical step. Start small. Begin with a smile and a greeting. Ask a question and really listen to the answer. Don't be afraid to listen to a point of view with which you may strongly disagree. Listening does not signify assent. It only helps you to understand.

It may be tempting to dismiss questions of identity and the church's struggle over its own diversity as a cultural fad or an exercise in political correctness. But Scripture indicates that diversity is part of God's design. The struggles we face over our differences are a by-product not only of the fall but of God's ongoing redemptive work as well. Both our differences and our unity are gifts from God. The struggle to uphold our unity while honoring our unique identities is as much a part of God's enduring work of sanctification as it is a matter of our own determined obedience. We want to find an elegant answer that resolves all the problems that our differences create in five easy steps. If such a "simple" solution exists, it is surely a matter of confident faith in God's unfolding purpose for the church combined with an unbending commitment to the truth of His Word and our own obedience to it. This threefold commitment is not elegant, but messy. It does not lend itself easily to five-step solutions or one-size-fits-all strategies that can be implemented with little to no personal cost. Nor do such commitments shield us from our own mistakes or the criticism of others.

How can the church be all together different? Only by relying upon God's grace and by patiently dealing with our mutual sins and imperfections. This is accomplished by practicing the grace-filled and Spirit-empowered discipline of muddling through. The way forward is rocky, and it's certain that we will stumble along the way. But the ultimate destination is also certain. In the end, we will see all things as they truly are and be everything that we are supposed to be. "When Christ appears, we shall be like him, for we shall see him as he is" (1 John 3:2).

Questions for Reflection

1. Which of the areas of difference discussed in this book is most pressing in your life right now? Which is most pressing in your church?

2. How might your church provide a "table" where congregational differences can be explored and understood? How might God use you to get it started?

3. How would you respond to someone who said that cultural diversity is just a passing fad or too difficult to achieve?

4. What is the next thing you feel God wants you to do in order to respond to what you have learned?

GLOSSARY

The following terms are used throughout the book and build on the standard definitions within the discipline of social psychology. Specific guidance came from S. Alexander Haslam, Stephen D. Reicher, and Michael J. Platow, *The New Psychology of Leadership*. The definitions here are designed for the general reader and should not be taken as precise clinical meanings. They are written in order to facilitate understanding for those unfamiliar with social psychology generally and social identity theory specifically. (Often more technical definitions with citations occur in the body of our book.)

Categorization. A process in which two or more things are seen along the lines of similarity and difference in a specific context. This is a central cognitive process for identity formation.

Cognitive Miser. A process of lazy categorizations. It accounts for the presence of limited thinking based on learned shortcuts. The alternative is cognitive generosity, in which categorizations that are found to be inaccurate are engaged constructively, resulting in new ways of thinking about difference and conflict resolution.

Cognitive Structure. The mindset or schema that allows an identity performance or action. See **Identity Salience**.

Collective Behavior. Actions determined by group membership and performed in alignment with those members. Social identity allows collective action to occur, both in the mundane and dramatic.

Comparative Fit. A categorization principle that suggests a given category is more likely to become salient when differences between category members are seen to be less than those associated with a particular comparison outgroup.

Cross-Cutting Identities. These are social identities that cut across two or more identity hierarchies. They may function independently of one another until they come into conflict.

Depersonalization. A process of self-stereotyping in which the person understands him or herself to be a substitutable part or category member of a group. A key process in identifications.

Dual Identity. An approach to identity formation and conflict resolution that recognizes the continued salience of subgroup identities amid the formation of a superordinate one. It can include more than one subgroup identity, but the main point is the recognition of the dual nature of group identity. See **Meta-Contrast**, **Normative Fit**, and **Comparative Fit**.

Entrepreneur. In identity-based leadership studies, this type of leader pursues new and creative ways to solve old problems. This type of leader seeks to (a) create identity by offering alternative visions to the status quo, (b) coordinate identity by engaging in group experiences, and (c) mobilize identity by showing the everyday usefulness of it.

Future Identities. Narratives that groups create that connect the group's past, present, and future. The temporal orientation of the group has a significant impact on its identity. Possible future social identities play a key role in maintaining a group, since it impacts motivation and behavior. Identity problems are often over the future direction of the group.

Group. A collection of people who perceive themselves to share valuable characteristics, evaluations, and emotions by which they define themselves.

Group Norms. Generally-agreed-upon standards of behavior and social identifications among a specific group.

Groupthink. A process of consensus seeking that results in a lack of critical reflection on a perspective or group norms.

Identity. The term used in this book to indicate that sense of who you are in the broadest way possible. The sum total of the factors that relate to and form a person. The big eight factors include: physical and mental characteristics, history, relationships, commitments, boundaries, fluidity and fixity, self-interpreting memories, and future-orientation.

Identity Hierarchy. The way various identities are organized. This scale can shift based on the situation, and more than one identity can occupy the same spot in the hierarchy.

Identity Narrative. The story that a person or a group tells themselves in order to make sense of the world. See **Future Identities**.

Identity Salience. The likelihood that a given identity will be activated in a given situation. It is an identity that is ready to be acted upon.

Ingroup. A self-defining group in a particular setting.

Intergroup. Refers to interactions (often conflict based) and behaviors between members of different groups.

Interpersonal. Relational interactions between two or more people. See **Depersonalization**.

Intragroup. Refers to relationships (positively or negatively) and behaviors between members of the same group.

Master Identity. An identity that has high salience (is ready to be acted upon) and strong commitment that combine to strengthen personal identity. See **Superordinate Identity**.

Meta-Contrast. A categorization principle related to an increased recognition of similarity within a group as well as an increased differentiation between that ingroup and another specific outgroup.

Nested Identities. Social identities nested under a superordinate one.

Normative Fit. A categorization principle highlighting the idea that a given category is more likely to become salient when there is an observation that certain patterns of behavior are consistent with what was previously expected of the given group members.

Outgroup. A non-self-defining group in a particular setting.

Personal Identity. A person's knowledge that they are different from other people in a group that is highlighted further by unique values that make them distinct from others in the group. Used interchangeably with "individual identity."

Prototype. Refers to the way a group member represents the given category in view. A prototypical leader embodies what the group values, its shared ingroup prototype. An ingroup prototype relates to common features that define the ingroup, while an outgroup stereotype highlights common features magnified in order to define the outgroup.

Self-Categorization. A process in which a person views themselves as a switchable category member who can be defined at different levels—personal or social.

Shared Group Beliefs. Convictions among group members that are evident to them and represent what it means to be part of the group. They provide the mental image for that which unifies the group. They foster the ingroup and outgroup boundary-marking process.

Social Categorization. A process in which multiple people are perceived in light of their similarities and differences in a particular setting.

Social Identification. Focuses on the various processes that give rise to a social identity, such as social categorization. It highlights the ongoing and processual nature of identity and the way it can shift based on changing contexts. Identification has cognitive, evaluative, and emotional elements to it.

Social Identity. That part of an individual's self-concept that emerges from their group memberships and the values associated with those memberships. Used interchangeably with group identity.

Social Identity Approach to Leadership. A process of influencing group members to achieve the group's goals. This is a unique approach to leadership that is informed significantly by the continuation of existing identities in shared group goal achievement and negotiation. The focus is on the group, not the individual leader's traits. Good leaders are ascribed this status by the group as they embody the shared group prototype. See also **Dual Identity.**

Social Identity Performance. The visible, social expression of one's sense of belonging to a particular group.

Social Identity Theory. A meta-theory developed by Henri Tajfel and John C. Turner that helps to explain intergroup and intragroup relations along with social conflict.

Social Influence. A process by which key people contribute to the formation of identity by changing attitudes and behaviors. Communication and language are key forms of this.

Stereotype. A representation of a group that is shared by its members or other groups.

Subgroup. A smaller group within a larger one that organizes itself along the lines of certain unique characteristics or traits considered valuable and useful. See **Dual Identity**.

Superordinate Identity. An overarching shared social identity formed via ongoing comparisons and relationships. This defines the outgroup and reinforces the ingroup. It is similar to a common or overarching identity. See **Master Identity**.

NOTES

Chapter 1: Our Identity Crisis

1. Marian Salzman, "Should Branding Begin at Birth?," Forbes, January 8, 2013, http://www.forbes.com/sites/mariansalzman/2013/01/08/when-should-branding-begin/#7ab6a8b97116.

2. Tom Peters, "The Brand Called You: You Can't Move Up if You Don't Stand Out," *Fast Company*, August 31, 1997, https://www.fastcompany.com/28905/brand-called-you.

3. Wesley Morris, "The Year We Obsessed Over Identity," *New York Times*, October 6, 2015.

4. Ibid.

5. Ibid.

6. Evan Urqhart, "It Isn't Crazy to Compare Rachel Dolezal with Caitlyn Jenner," http://www.slate.com/blogs/outward/2015/06/15/rachel_dolezal_caitlyn_jenner_how_transgender_is_different_from_transracial.html.

7. Ibid.

8. D. C. McAllister, "Why Bruce Jenner Can Never Be a Woman," http://thefederalist.com/2015/06/04/why-bruce-jenner-can-never-be-a-woman/.

9. Ibid.

10. Deborah Tannen, *You Just Don't Understand: Women and Men in Conversation* (New York: Ballantine, 1990), 15–16.

11. Ibid., 16.

12. J. Richard Middleton, *The Liberating Image: The IMAGO DEI in Genesis 1* (Grand Rapids: Brazos, 2005), 27.

13. Peter Berger, *The Sacred Canopy: Elements of a Sociological Theory of Religion* (New York: Anchor, 1967), 6.

14. Ibid.

15. Ibid., 7.

16. Craig Storti, *The Art of Crossing Cultures* (Yarmouth: Intercultural Press, 1990), 52.

17. Ibid.

18. Ibid., 48.

Chapter 2: Seeing Ourselves in God's Mirror

1. David Brooks, *The Road To Character* (New York: Random House, 2015), 61.

2. Ibid.

3. Ibid., 68.

4. Stanley J. Grenz, *The Social God and the Relational Self* (Louisville: Westminster John Knox, 2001), 99.

5. Charles Taylor, *Sources of the Self: The Making of Modern Identity* (Cambridge: Harvard, 1989), 50.

6. Ibid.

7. Anne Lamott, *Bird by Bird: Some Instructions on Writing and Life* (New York: Anchor, 1994), 56.

8. Taylor, *Sources of the Self*, 51.

9. Klyne R. Snodgrass, "Introduction to a Hermeneutics of Identity," *Bibliotheca Sacra* 168 (January–March 2011): 5.

10. Ibid.

11. Andy Crouch, *Culture Making* (Downers Grove: InterVarsity, 2008), 23.

12. C. S. Lewis, *Mere Christianity* (New York: Macmillan, 1952), 38.

13. Ibid.

14. Marcus Johnson, *One With Christ: An Evangelical Theology of Salvation* (Wheaton: Crossway, 2013), 123.

Chapter 3: I Am the Walrus

1. S. Alexander Haslam, Stephen D. Reicher, and Michael J. Platow, *The New Psychology of Leadership: Identity, Influence, and Power* (New York: Psychology, 2011), 249.

2. Klyne R. Snodgrass, "Introduction to a Hermeneutics of Identity," *Bibliotheca Sacra* 168 (January–March 2011): 11–13.

3. Ibid.

4. Gary Burge, *Jesus and the Land* (Grand Rapids: Baker, 2010), 59.

5. Mark Kinzer, "Zionism in Luke-Acts," in *The New Christian Zionism: Fresh Perspectives on Israel and the Land*, ed. Gerald R. McDermott

(Downers Grove: InterVarsity, 2016), 140–65, offers a critique of Burge for those interested.

6. James D. G. Dunn, *The Theology of Paul the Apostle* (Grand Rapids: Eerdmans, 1998), 397–398.

7. Ibid., 401.

8. W. D. Davies, *Paul and Rabbinic Judaism* (Philadelphia: Fortress, 1980), 86.

9. Ibid., 90.

10. William S. Campbell, *Paul and the Creation of Christian Identity* (London: T&T Clark, 2006), 156.

11. S. Alexander Haslam, *Psychology in Organizations: A Social Identity Approach* (London: Sage, 2004), 281.

12. Ibid., 280.

13. Ben Witherington, *Conflict and Community* (Grand Rapids: Eerdmans, 1995), 295–98.

14. Christena Cleveland, *Disunity in Christ* (Downers Grove: IVP, 2013), 62.

Chapter 4: In with the "In Crowd"

1. S. Alexander Haslam, *Psychology in Organizations: A Social Identity Approach* (London: Sage, 2004), 281.

2. Henri Tajfel and John C. Turner, "An Integrative Theory of Group Conflict," in *The Social Psychology of Intergroup Relations*, eds. W. G. Austin and S. Worchel (Monterey, CA: Brooks/Cole, 1979), 40. See J. Brian Tucker and Coleman A. Baker, eds., *T&T Clark Handbook to Social Identity in the New Testament* (London: Bloomsbury T&T Clark, 2016) for a full detailing on social identity theory and how it works in the New Testament.

3. https://www.theguardian.com/stage/2005/sep/29/comedy.religion.

4. Christena Cleveland, *Disunity in Christ* (Downers Grove: InterVarsity, 2013), 33. She also highlights a different version of this joke.

5. Michael Hogg and Dominic Abrams, *Social Identifications: A Social Psychology of Intergroup Relations and Group Processes* (London: Routledge, 1988), 3.

6. Ibid., 4–5.

7. J. Brian Tucker, "The Over-Churched: Preaching to People Who Have 'Heard It All Before,'" *The Journal of Ministry and Theology* 6 (2003): 69–90.

8. J. Brian Tucker, "Doctrine-Aware Sermons: Preaching Doctrinally-Informed and Relationally-Connected Messages," *The Journal of Ministry and Theology* 11 (Spring 2007): 124–44.

9. J. Brian Tucker, *"You Belong to Christ": Paul and the Formation of Social Identity in 1 Corinthians 1–4* (Eugene: Pickwick, 2010), 2.

10. J. Brian Tucker, "Religious Leaders: New Testament," in *The Oxford Encyclopedia of the Bible and Gender Studies*, ed. Julia M. O'Brien (New York: Oxford University Press, 2014), 184–89.

11. Haslam, *Psychology in Organizations*, 282.

12. Daniel Bar-Tal, *Group Beliefs* (New York: Springer, 1990), 39.

13. J. Brian Tucker, *Reading 1 Corinthians* (Eugene: Cascade, 2017), 124–32.

14. Kathy Ehrensperger, *Paul at the Crossroads of Cultures* (London: Bloomsbury, 2013), 1–13.

15. Jack Barentsen, *Emerging Leadership in the Pauline Mission: A Social Identity Perspective on Local Leadership Development in Corinth and Ephesus* (Eugene: Pickwick, 2011), 83–85.

16. Steven Garber, *The Fabric of Faithfulness: Weaving Together Belief and Behavior* (Downers Grove: InterVarsity, 2007), 176; John Stonestreet and Brent Kunkle, *A Practical Guide to Culture* (Colorado Springs: David C. Cook, 2017).

17. Inge Jens, ed., *At the Heart of the White Rose: Letters and Diaries of Hans and Sophie Scholl* (New York: Harper & Row, 1987), 115.

18. Ibid., xii; Steven Garber, *The Fabric of Faithfulness: Weaving Together Belief and Behavior* (Downers Grove: InterVarsity, 2007), 178.

19. Garber, *The Fabric of Faithfulness*, 180.

20. J. Brian Tucker, *"Remain in Your Calling": Paul and the Continuation of Social Identities in 1 Corinthians* (Eugene: Pickwick, 2011), 19–22.

21. Scott Bartchy, "Paulus hat nicht gelehrt: 'Jeder soll in seinem Stand bleiben' Luthers Fehlübersetzung von *klesis* in 1. Korinther 7," in *Alte texte in neuen kontexten: wo steht die sozialwissenschaftliche exegese?*, eds. Wolfgang Stegeman and Richard DeMaris (Stuttgart: Kohlhammer, 2010), 234, 237.

22. Ibid., 238–39.

23. Marvin J. Newell, *Crossing Cultures in Scripture: Biblical Principles for Mission Practice* (Downers Grove: InterVarsity, 2016), 247.

24. David J. Rudolph, *A Jew to the Jews: Jewish Contours of Pauline Flexibility in 1 Corinthians 9:19–23* (Eugene: Pickwich, 2016), 165, italics original; Gal. 6:2.

25. Ibid., 166.

26. J. Brian Tucker, "The Jerusalem Collection, Economic Inequality, and Human Flourishing: Is Paul's Concern the Redistribution of Wealth, or a Relationship of Mutuality (or Both)?," *Canadian Theological Review* (2014): 59–62.

27. Leroy Barber, *Embrace: God's Radical Shalom for a Divided World* (Downers Grove: InterVarsity, 2016), 28–30.

28. Ibid., 30.

Chapter 5: One among Many

1. Dionysius of Halicarnassus, *Roman Antiquities IV*, trans. Earnest Cary, Loeb Classical Library 364 (Cambridge: Harvard University Press, 1943), 55–57.

2. Kar Yong Lim, *Metaphors and Social Identity Formation* (Eugene: Pickwick, 2017), 184.

3. J. Todd Billings, *Union with Christ: Reframing Theology and Ministry for the Church* (Grand Rapids: Baker, 2014), 1.

4. N. Ellemers, P. Kortekaas, and J.W. Ouwerkerk, "Self-categorization, Commitment to the Group, and Group Self-esteem as Related but Distinct Aspects of Social Identity," *European Journal of Social Psychology* 29 (1999): 372.

5. William S. Campbell, "Paul and Union with Christ: Theological Approaches and the Fossilization of Christian Identity" (paper presented at the annual meeting of the Institute for Biblical Research, Baltimore, MD, November 23–26, 2013), 8.

6. Gilles Fauconnier, *Mappings in Thought and Language* (Cambridge: CUP, 1997); George Lakoff and Mark Johnson, *Metaphors We Live By* (Chicago: UCP, 1980), 6, 66–67, 83.

7. Christena Cleveland, *Disunity in Christ* (Downers Grove: InterVarsity, 2013), 178–86.

8. Ben Dunson, *Individual and Community in Paul's Letter to the Romans* (Tübingen, Germany: Mohr Siebeck, 2011), 16.

9. N. T. Wright, *Paul and the Faithfulness of God* (Minneapolis: Fortress, 2013), 3–74.

10. Timothy Keller, *Making Sense of God* (New York: Penguin, 2016), 150.

11. S. L. Gaertner, M. C. Rust, J. F. Dovidio, B. A. Bachman, and P. A. Anastasio, "The Contact Hypothesis: The Role of Common I ngroup Identity on Reducing Intergroup Bias among Majority and Minority Group Members," in *What's Social About Social Cognition?: Research on Socially Shared Cognition in Small Groups*, eds. J. L. Nye and A. M. Brower (Newbury Park: Sage, 1996), 232.

12. M. B. Brewer, "Superordinate Goals versus Superordinate Identity as Bases of Intergroup Cooperation," in *Social Identity Processes: Trends in Theory and Research*, eds. D. Capozza and R. Brown (London: Sage, 2000), 119.

13. S. A. Haslam, *Psychology in Organizations: The Social Identity Approach* (London: Sage, 2004), 127.

14. But see Douglas. J. Moo, *The Letters to the Colossians and to Philemon* (Grand Rapids: Eerdmans, 2008), 421 n. 92, who offers nuanced comments on the significance of this issue. For further discussion on the grammar in verse 16 and the broader argument in Philemon, see J. Brian Tucker, "Paul's Particular Problem—The Continuation of Existing Identities in Philemon" in *T&T Clark Handbook to Social Identity in the New Testament*, eds. J. Brian Tucker and Coleman A. Baker (London: Bloomsbury T&T Clark, 2013), 413–16.

15. P. Lampe, "Affects and Emotions in the Rhetoric of Paul's Letter to Philemon," in *Philemon in Perspective: Interpreting a Pauline Letter*, ed. D. F. Tolmie (Berlin: De Gruyter, 2010), 61–77.

16. Haslam, *Psychology in Organizations*, 127–28.

17. Against J. G. Nordling, *Philemon* (Saint Louis: Concordia, 2004), 258.

18. Cleveland, *Disunity in Christ*, 158.

19. Thomas Howard, *Evangelical Is Not Enough* (Nashville: Thomas Nelson, 1984), 36.

Chapter 6: Race, Ethnicity, and Identity

1. R. Albert Mohler Jr., "Conceived in Sin, Called by the Gospel," in *Removing the Stain of Racism from the Southern Baptist Convention*, eds. Jarvis J. Williams and Kevin M. Jones (Nashville: B&H, 2017), 4.

2. Eric Geiger, *Identity: Who You Are in Christ* (Nashville: B&H, 2008), 8.

3. Tony Evans, *Oneness Embraced* (Chicago: Moody, 2011), 44–45.

4. Timothy Keller, *Making Sense of God* (New York: Penguin, 2016), 150.

5. Finney Philip, "1 Corinthians," in *South Asia Bible Commentary*, ed. Brian Wintle (Grand Rapids: Zondervan, 2015), 1576.

6. Andrew T. Lincoln, *Ephesians* (Nashville: Thomas Nelson, 1990), 143–44; Minna Shkul, *Reading Ephesians* (London: T&T Clark, 2009), 125.

7. Evans, *Oneness Embraced*, 44. For an example of an erasure interpreter, see Andrew T. Lincoln, *Ephesians* (Nashville: Thomas Nelson, 1990), 144.

8. Justin Hardin, "Equality in the Church," in *Introduction to Messianic Judaism*, eds. David Rudolph and Joel Willitts (Grand Rapids: Zondervan, 2013), 229–32.

9. Markus Barth, *Israel and the Church: Contribution to a Dialogue Vital for Peace* (Richmond: John Knox Press, 1969), 89–90.

10. Markus Barth, *Ephesians* (Garden City: Doubleday, 1974), 310.

11. Richard Twiss, *Rescuing the Gospel from the Cowboys* (Downers Grove: InterVarsity, 2015), 104.

12. For several practical steps in moving toward racial reconciliation more broadly based on Ephesians 2, see the fifteen steps offered by Jarvis J. Williams, "Biblical Steps," in *Removing the Stain of Racism*, 45–51.

13. See further for a similar list Angela M. Sabates, *Social Psychology in Christian Perspective* (Downers Grove: InterVarsity, 2012), 370–72, who builds on Curtiss Paul DeYoung, *Coming Together in the 21st Century* (Valley Forge: Judson Press, 2009).

Chapter 7: Neither Male nor Female

1. Diane E. Levin and Jean Kilbourne, *So Sexy So Soon: The New Sexualized Childhood and What Parents Can Do to Protect Their Kids* (New York: Ballantine, 2008), 16.

2. Jean Kilbourne, "Jesus Is a Pair of Jeans," *New Internationalist*, September 2006, 11.

3. Ibid., 12.

4. Richard Middleton, *The Liberating Image: The Imago Dei in Genesis 1* (Grand Rapids: Brazos, 2005), 50.

5. Karl Barth, *Ethics* (New York: Seabury, 1981), 182–183.

6. Ibid., 183.

7. Barna Research Group, "What Americans Believe about Sex," January 14, 2016, https://www.barna.com/research/what-americans-believe -about-sex/.

8. Ibid.

9. Dale Kuehne, *Sex and the iWorld* (Grand Rapids: Baker, 2009), 79.

10. Ibid., 78.

11. Ibid., 169.

12. Jonathan Grant, *Divine Sex: A Compelling Vision for Christian Relationships in a Hypersexualized Age* (Grand Rapids: Brazos, 2015), 97.

13. Ibid., 197.

14. Ibid., 198.

15. Ibid.

16. Kuehne, *Sex and the iWorld*, 140.

17. Middleton, *The Liberating Image*, 50.

18. Stanley J. Grenz, *The Social God and the Relational Self: A Trini-
tarian Theology of the Imago Dei* (Louisville: Westminster John Knox,
2001), 280.

19. Ibid.

20. Ibid.

21. Donald G. Bloesch, *The Church: Sacraments, Worship, Ministry,
Mission* (Downers Grove: InterVarsity, 2002), 222.

22. Ibid., 222–223.

23. F. F. Bruce, *The Epistle to the Galatians* (Grand Rapids: Eerdmans,
1982), 187.

24. Helmut Thielicke, *The Ethics of Sex* (New York: Harper & Row,
1964), 23.

25. Ibid., 21.

26. Alice Matthews, *Preaching that Speaks to Women* (Grand Rapids:
Baker, 2003), 54.

27. Ibid., 53.

28. Rosaria Champagne Butterfield, *The Secret Thoughts of an Unlikely
Convert: An English Professor's Journey into Christian Faith* (Pitts-
burgh: Crown & Covenant, 2012), 23.

29. Ibid.

30. Charles Taylor, *A Secular Age* (Cambridge: Belknap, 2007), 767.

Chapter 8: Generational Differences

1. Ed Stetzer, "Generational Impact: How Generational Dynamics Impact Our Evangelism," ChristianityToday.com, http://www
.christianitytoday.com/edstetzer/2016/october/does-it-really-matter
-how-generational-dynamics-impact-our-.html.

2. "The First Generation of the Twenty-First Century: An Introduction to the Pluralist Generation," Magid Generational Strategies, http://magid.com/sites/default/files/pdf/MagidPluralistGenerationWhite paper.pdf.

3. Carson Nyquist, email to the author, February 8, 2015.

4. Mark Aardsma, phone conversation with the author.

5. Kerwin Rodriguez, personal conversation with the author.

6. Leila Canaan Messarra, Silva Karkoulian, and Abdul-Nasser El-Kassar, "Conflict Resolution Styles and Personality," in *International Journal of Productivity and Performance Management* no. 65, no. 6 (2016) 792–810.

7. Mark Aardsma, phone conversation with the author.

8. Paul Taylor, *The Next America: Boomers, Millennials, and the Looming Generational Showdown* (New York: Public-Affairs, 2014), 20.

9. Ibid.

10. D'Vera Cohn and Paul Taylor, "Baby Boomers Approach 65–Glumly," Pew Research Center, December 20, 2010, http://www.pew socialtrends.org/2010/12/20/baby-boomers-approach-65-glumly/.

11. Jerell Carper, email to the author.

12. Paul Taylor and George Gao, "Generation X: America's Neglected Middle Child," http://www.pewresearch.org/fact-tank/2014/06/05/generation-x-americas-neglected-middle-child/.

13. Timothy Tseng, "Asian American Religious Leadership Today: A Preliminary Inquiry," *Pulpit & Pew Research on Pastoral Leadership* (Durham: Duke Divinity School, 2006), 24.

14. Ibid.

15. Edwin J. Hernández, Milagros Peña, Rev. Kenneth Davis, CSC, and Elizabeth Station, "Strengthening Hispanic Ministry across Denominations: A Call to Action," *Pulpit & Pew Research on Pastoral Leadership* (Durham: Duke Divinity School, 2005), 8.

16. Ibid.

17. Julio Guarneri, "Five Greats for Leaders of Hispanic Churches," *Christianity Today*, http://www.christianitytoday.com/ct/en-espanol/five-greats-for-leaders-of-hispanic-churches.html.

18. Ibid.

19. Ibid.

20. Ibid.

21. Pew Research Center, "A Religious Portrait of African Americans," http://www.pewforum.org/2009/01/30/a-religious-portrait-of-african -americans/.

22. Larry Mamiya, "River of Struggle, River of Freedom: Trends among Black Churches and Black Pastoral Leadership," *Pulpit & Pew Research on Pastoral Leadership* (Durham: Duke Divinity School, 2006), 24.

23. Ibid., 25.

24. Ibid.

25. Ibid., 30–31.

26. Barna Group, "The State of Pastors," 2017, 11–12.

27. The Barna Group, "The Aging of America's Pastors," March 1, 2017, https://www.barna.com/research/aging-americas-pastors/.

28. Ibid.

29. Andrew C. Thompson, "Community or Institution? To Gen X, the Answer Should Be Obvious," in *Faith & Leadership*, February 9, 2009, https://www.faithandleadership.com/content/community-or -institution-gen-x-the-answer-should-be-obvious.

30. Ibid.

31. Sam Hannom, email to the author, February 9, 2015.

32. Dietrich Bonhoeffer, *Life Together* (New York: HarperOne, 1954), 19.

33. Ibid., 27.

34. Ibid., 21.

Chapter 9: Living like Outsiders—Accepting Our Alien Identity

1. Rod Dreher, "The Idea of a Christian Village," *Christianity Today*, March 2017, 36.

2. Ibid.

3. C. S. Lewis, *Mere Christianity* (San Francisco: HarperOne, 1952), 210.

4. James K. A. Smith, *Desiring the Kingdom: Worship, Worldview, and Cultural Formation* (Grand Rapids: Baker, 2009), 90.

5. Ibid., 93.

6. Ibid., 103.

7. William A. Dyrness, *How Does America Hear the Gospel?* (Grand Rapids: Eerdmans, 1989), 100.

8. F. F. Bruce, *The Acts of the Apostles* (Grand Rapids: Eerdmans, 1951), 75.

9. Donald K. Smith, *Creating Understanding: A Handbook for Christian Communication Across Cultural Landscapes* (Grand Rapids: Zondervan, 1992), 254.

Chapter 10: Final Thoughts

1. Andy Crouch, *Culture Making: Recovering Our Creative Calling* (Downers Grove: InterVarsity, 2013), 28.

ACKNOWLEDGMENTS

From Brian

I would like to thank John for catching a vision for this book and for seeing the way culture, identity, and ministry are interconnected. Your willingness to see these connections breathed new life into this research. Thanks for your partnership. I would like to thank my students, colleagues, and administrators for providing an environment in which these ideas could flourish. I am always grateful for the way my family continues to provide insights into life together. Thanks, Amber, Ashley and Matt, Alexandria and John, Annaliese, and Abigail. Your love and support are constantly felt.

From John

I would like to thank Brian for being the brains of this project. The vision for this project was sparked by your work in this area. I am grateful to my students in the course Cultural Dynamics of Congregational Ministry for wrestling with me as we have had the pleasure of reflecting on the mysteries of culture, difference, and congregational life for more than two decades. I am especially thankful for my wife, Jane, who is always my first editor, best critic, and greatest advocate for all that I write.

From Brian and John

We are grateful to Drew Dyck, whose passion for this book early on was inspiring. To our agent, Mark Sweeney, whose tireless effort behind the scenes helped make this project possible. And finally to Kevin Emmert, whose editorial insights resulted in a more focused, enjoyable, and readable book.

A practical guide to walking with low-income people

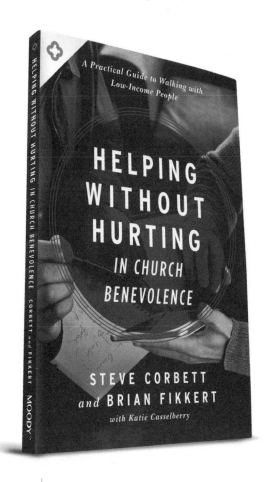

*A short guide to living, leading,
and ministering as a pastor*